LIVE WELL IN HONDURAS

HOW TO RELOCATE, RETIRE, AND INCREASE YOUR STANDARD OF LIVING

Frank Ford

John Muir Publications
Santa Fe, New Mexico

99

John Muir Publications, P.O. Box 613, Santa Fe, New Mexico 87504

Printed in the United States of America
First edition. First printing September 1998

Library of Congress Cataloging-in-Publication Data

Ford, Frank, 1920–
    Live well in Honduras: how to relocate, retire, and increase your standard
of living / Frank Ford. – 1st ed.
    p. cm.
    Includes index.
    ISBN 1-56261-339-1
    1. Honduras—Guidebooks. 2. Retirement, Places of—Honduras—
Guidebooks. 3. Investments, American—Honduras—Guidebooks.
I. Title.
F1503.5.F67 1998
972.83—DC21   97-44102
                                                                      CIP

Editors: Peg Goldstein, Chris Hayhurst, Dianna Delling
Production: Marie J. T. Vigil, Nikki Rooker
Interior Design: Marie J. T. Vigil
Cover Design: Linda Harper
Typesetting: Kathleen Sparkes, White Hart Design
Map Illustration: Kathleen Sparkes, White Hart Design
Printer: Publishers Press
Front Cover Photo: James D. Gollin
Back Cover Photo: top—Leo de Wys Inc./Randy Taylor
                  bottom—James D. Gollin

Distributed to the book trade by
Publishers Group West
Berkeley, California

Contents

▼▲▼

Preface

▼▲▼

This is a retirement book, but it is not directed solely at the senior citizen who has just received the gold-watch farewell. Instead it is written for all people who are thinking of retiring from their present situation, including those who wish to work in a new enterprise, using old skills in a fresh field with a new horizon.

Nor is this book a solo effort, although it includes personal anecdotes and is guided by a personal point of view. This book is a collaborative effort, the result of interviews with dozens of foreign retirees in Honduras and of casual conversations with many others—native and foreign, tour guides and tour owners, hoteliers and cabbies, desk clerks and bellhops. Most of all, I have called on the many resources of *International Living*, an influential monthly publication, based in Baltimore, that features beauties and bargains the world over. I am especially indebted to Barbara Pariello, one of *International Living*'s travel experts in Delray Beach, Florida.

This book concerns residing, retiring, and investing in Honduras. It discusses the country's many advantages and the few inevitable drawbacks. It tries to warn off those who might find the country incompatible with their temperament or habits, and it attempts to ease the adjustment of those who do decide to make the move.

Because this book is published in the United States, I sometimes use "Americans" to designate my fellow U.S. citizens. Latin America has devised an excellent word, *estadounidense*, but its translation, "United Stateser," is too clumsy. By using the word Americans, I do not mean to exclude our Canadian neighbors, to whom I hope this book will be equally serviceable, nor anyone else in North or South America.

The term "Central America" does not include Mexico, which its neighbors call "Middle America." Mexico has always seemed to the Latins a distinct and powerful entity. Central America comprises the five countries to the south of Mexico, the five "provinces" that declared their independence from Spain in 1821: Guatemala,

Honduras, El Salvador, Nicaragua, and Panama. The flag of
Honduras recalls this historic break: On a white stripe between two
blue stripes are emblazoned five stars in honor of the five provinces.

Because I am a former English teacher, I cannot in good con-
science use *they* to refer to a singular noun such as retiree or investor.
As an old codger resistant to ugly trends, I hate the hybrids *he/she,*
her/his, and *him/her.* Therefore, to my female readers, of whom I
hope there will be many, I apologize for my old-fashioned use of *he,*
his, and *him* and assure them that no sexual bias is intended.

This book does not assume that the reader has a knowledge of
Spanish. Occasionally I use Spanish words like *Ladino* or *mestizo,*
where either no English equivalent exists or where an English substitute might be misleading. Sometimes Spanish words tag along in
parentheses to help readers identify words they may see on signs, hear
in gas stations, or find in legal documents. One chapter discusses the
extent to which Spanish is needed in different parts of the country
and offers hints to help the traveler who has little or no Spanish.

Because this book is aimed primarily at North Americans, it uses
such terms as *feet, yards, miles,* and *acres.* But before you leave for a
trip to Central America, please familiarize yourself with the table of
metric conversions in the back of this book, because most measurements you will encounter in Honduras will be metric.

I have enjoyed the challenge of presenting an honest picture of
a sleeping giant of a country just beginning to rouse from a five-
century slumber—a land of great beauty, charm, Edenic pleasures,
and vast opportunity. I hope you find the following pages valuable.
I would enjoy hearing your comments, questions, or suggestions;
you can write to me care of John Muir Publications, P.O. Box 613,
Santa Fe, NM 87504.

▼▲▼▲▼▲▼▲▼▲▼▲▼▲▼▲▼▲▼▲▼▲▼▲▼▲▼▲▼▲▼▲▼▲▼▲▼▲▼

Southward to Eden

D o you dream? In color? I mean, when you're awake? During an icebound winter, do you dream of cosseting warmth and radiant sunshine? In bumper-to-bumper traffic on a jammed freeway or a gridlocked city street, do you long for a less congested area, a place of quiet and tranquillity? In an age of terrorism, do you wish for a country that no one hates enough to terrorize?

When credit cards bite the hand that feeds them, bills become mountains, and debts endless deserts, when the midnight oil burnt to deal with them seems an environmental disaster, do you long for a life without stress and find yourself muttering with Thoreau: "Simplify! Simplify!"?

We all do. When routine becomes deadening and familiar surroundings seem drab and dull, we all ache for the adventure of change and difference, the intoxication of strange and exotic beauty.

That's when we often dream of a tropical paradise. Of Xanadu. Shangri La. The yellow brick road to Oz. The rainbow bridge to

Valhalla and Asgard. But sober reflection tells us that these are impossible dreams.

Yet, what about the *possible* dream?

A dream of an idyllic life in a warm and friendly country far from snow and icy wintry blasts, of lolling in a hammock while a smiling maid servant fetches cool drinks and a skillful groundskeeper brings forth a profusion of exotic flowers and fresh vegetables from your small estate; and all for less than half of what a much simpler lifestyle would cost in the United States.

Or—for dreamers too young for retirement—a dream of a new and active life, directing a new business, employing grateful workers in a country welcoming your contribution to its well-being and making advantageous concessions to ensure your stay.

The possible dream! Many of your compatriots can assure you that these Technicolor dreams can be realized—and not very far away. Just start looking, they say, south of the border. Crossing the Rio Grande is the right move. But not all the countries you'll encounter there are, at present, equally desirable.

Mexico

For more than a generation, Mexico lured Americans retiring with limited income, and thousands of retirees heeded the call. But, on the day the North American Free Trade Agreement (NAFTA) became a reality, New Year's Day 1994, Mexico was no longer such a safe and serene harbor.

Rebellious Zapatistas stormed out of the mountains, seized a town, and exposed widespread unappeased hungers. The assassination of the leading presidential candidate, still unsolved, shocked the country. Somewhat later, the peso collapsed disastrously, causing a loss of about $40 billion and 2 million Mexican jobs. Inflation soared, impoverishing millions of the country's citizens.

Mexico startled financial circles in 1997 by early repayment of a controversial $13.5 billion U.S. loan to stave off default. The punishment of the peso had made Mexico's exports worldwide bargains and grew the gross national product by 5 percent in each of the next two years. That was good news from our nation's third largest trading partner. But that one success served only as contrast to the general malaise.

The Mexican government, its corruption admittedly institutionalized (a kind of country-wide Tammany Hall), is vulnerable and floundering. The Institutional Revolutionary Party (PRI) is collapsing after 68 years of control. Since the elections of July 1997, the two major opposition parties in the Chamber of Deputies, when they choose to combine forces, can now muster enough votes to break the PRI's chokehold on the national budget. The hated increase of the sales tax to 15 percent is an issue inviting such joint action.

The powerful Salinas and other great political families are racked by scandals. The governors of the states of Sonora and Morales are on the U.S. blacklist as venal collaborators with drug lords. The new president, Ernesto Zedillo, had to arrest the head of Mexico's anti-narcotics program on drug charges. The shadowy Popular Revolutionary Army (EPR) remains active and violent in the state of Guerrero. As late as fall 1996, masked guerrillas were attacking police and government installations in five southern states in Mexico.

Civic turbulence has brought criminal chaos in its wake, with widespread reports of teenage mobsters, open assaults on the elderly, and vigilante justice in villages. Mexico's luster as a tourist haven has become tarnished. Travelers' eyes now often turn farther south.

Guatemala

Guatemala—"the land of eternal spring"—is a beautiful land offering an ideal climate. But the nation has been plagued by a series of repressive military governments and a 36-year conflict—Central America's longest and last civil war, marked by bloody repression, guerrilla assaults, pogroms against the Maya Indians and other indigenes, mutilations and terrorist explosions, and scorched-earth massacres of whole villages.

Over the years, retirees in Guatemala had to contend with outbreaks of violent anti-Americanism, fed by baseless tales of Americans stealing babies. Rumors of kidnappings for ransom further clouded the sunny clime. At long last, two days before the end of

1996, the guns fell silent, and a peace treaty was signed by the government under a civilian president and the Guatemalan National Revolutionary Unit.

But the wounds are fresh, the scars unhealed. At least 140,000 people were killed or "disappeared." More than 250,000 children were made orphans, and more than one million people were driven from their homes during the conflict. There is unrest and cynicism about the feasibility of the accords. Financially, the treaty creates severe problems. The cost of fulfilling its provisions runs into the billions, far beyond Guatemala's ability to pay. The country's infrastructure and most government agencies are in disrepair, impoverished by the voracity of the long-dominant war machine. And Guatemala's avian currency, the quetzal, its feathers singed, does not fly as far as it once did.

Belize and Costa Rica

Belize, with the advantage of English as its national language, and Costa Rica, with the most advanced democracy and most beautiful capital in Central America, both have enjoyed great popularity with tourists. But that very popularity has cost them dearly. The infrastructure, particularly in Belize, has not kept up, and inflation has soared. Recent legal changes have made residency in Costa Rica less advantageous. The cost of living there is now about the same as in Canada or the resort towns of Mexico.

As Peter Dickinson warns, "Once inflation in a country tops 15 percent, the local government often controls imports and exports of capital, possession of foreign bank accounts, ownership of gold, and foreign travel, and imposes other wage and price controls. And once inflation tops 30 percent a year, the local currency isn't worth even the paper it's printed on."[1]

Of course, the results of inflation are shortages of all kinds and more controls. This situation may not alarm the tourist who expects extravagance, but a person considering residency abroad may well be concerned. The benefits and privileges that once attracted retirees, especially the *pensionado* program, have been somewhat curtailed.

As Shelley Emling writes in *Your Guide to Retiring to Mexico, Costa Rica and Beyond*, "In some parts of Costa Rica, real estate values have been escalating by 100 percent a year. . . . Household belongings can no longer be imported into the country free. Instead they are taxed at a rate of 100 percent. An imported car here costs five times what it does in most other countries because of the exorbitant automobile tax of 520 percent. . . . A sales tax of 12 percent is added on the sale of merchandise or the billing of a service."[2]

As one merchant mariner who has lived in both Costa Rica and Honduras told me, "Costa just got too expensive." (I cringe to remember that I replied in stage-fake Italian, "You meana, Costa costa too much.")

El Salvador and Nicaragua

El Salvador and Nicaragua are known to the entire world—and for bad reason. The horrifying civil wars and bloody aftermaths have left bitter polarization and open wounds. Nicaragua, the largest Central American country, for decades has been notorious for savage internal strife. With the hostility of the United States, Contra harassment, and the arbitrariness of the Sandanistas and their unprecedented military buildup, the new government resulting from the 1990 free elections found that the national economy had slid to the cellar of Central America. Nicaragua's citizens are too weary to encourage tourism, and they recognize that it would not supply the economic base their country needs. Nor is the country's infrastructure ready for an influx.

El Salvador, a small, overpopulated country rocked for centuries by earthquakes and volcanoes, has also been devastated by years of carpet bombing. Not until 1992 was a cease-fire pact achieved between the U.S.-backed military government and the leftist FMLN. Now both sides attempt to settle their differences by the ballot in a relatively stable agreement.

The last two elections have given the presidency peacefully to non-Marxists, but it is worth noting that Hector Silva became

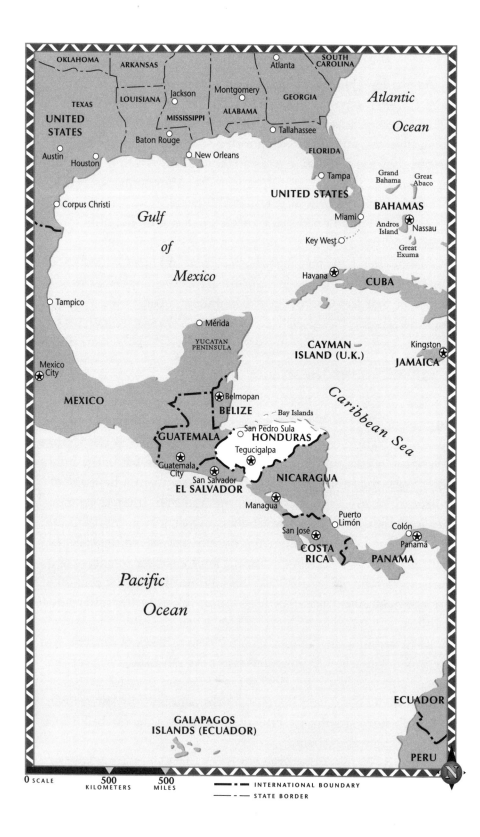

mayor of San Salvador, the capital, in spring 1997 and that the FMLN won a third of the seats in congress. Political differences are still abrasive, social tensions are still high, death-squad activity continues, unemployment is widespread, and the faltering economy leans on the fragile prop of AID dollars.

Panama

Panama? Nobody but Noriega yearns to go to that sweltering steam bath of a country. And more than a few Panamanians feel they have cause to resent Americans since "Operation Just Cause." To the historically minded, the country provided a shelf from which Balboa could "discover" the Pacific. To most seagoing foreigners it is a passageway between oceans. To Americans it is terrain around the Panama Canal, which we recently returned to the natives.

And the Winner Is . . .

Honduras. "Where exactly is Honduras?" the average American will ask. The original banana republic, the second largest country in Central America, is the third country down from the Rio Grande.

If you look just under Mexico on a map, you'll see the bust of a flat-headed Etch-a-Sketch soldier presenting his left profile. That's Guatemala, and it's appropriate to see it as a tin soldier, for that poor country has been run by the military most of the time. Cutting through the middle of the soldier's left shoulder is the western border of the inverted triangle that is Honduras, running diagonally down to meet the northern tip of El Salvador at the toy soldier's breastbone. Just below Honduras, on the other side of the tilted triangle, is Nicaragua.

> "Your heating budget alone in North Dakota would pay all expenses of comfortable living for a couple in Honduras."

There it is, Honduras, a wedge of peace among three

Glossary of Terms

Bay Islands (Islas de la Bahía): A group of islands off the North Coast of Honduras, including the largest islands of Roatán, Utila, and Guanaja

casas de cambio: exchange houses (places to exchange money)

centavo: $1/100$ of a lempira

Copán: The site of ruins of a major Mayan city in western Honduras

Daddy Warbucks investor: A foreign investor who pledges one million lempiras toward establishing a business in Honduras

Decree 80-92: Capstone of the new policy welcoming foreign investment

Decree 93-91: The principal Honduran law dealing with foreign pensionates and rentists

dispensa: The right of pensionates and rentists (and their dependents who are not investors) to bring their household furnishings to Honduras, exempt from customs duties and import taxes

estadounidense: Literally, a "United Stateser"; a citizen of the United States

FIDE: Foundation for Investments and Development of Exports (also known as the Industrial Development Group-Honduras); a nonprofit organization dedicated to nurturing the development of Honduran business

Free Zones: The cities of Puerto Cortés, Omoa, Choloma, Tela, La Ceiba, and Ampala. Export companies operating in these zones may import material, equipment, and office supplies without duties, and they are exempt from taxes. The companies may repatriate money without restriction.

Garifunas: Black Caribs; descendants of African slaves who intermarried with natives on the island of St. Vincent and were later deported to the Bay Islands. Garifunas still live on the Bay Islands and on Honduras's Caribbean coast

Hondutel: Government-run offices offering phone, fax, and internet services

jubilado: A retiree who has passed his 65th birthday

Ladino: A person of mestizo descent; the Honduran mestizo culture

lempira: The Honduran unit of currency. As of April 1998, the rate of exchange was 13.19L for $1.

mestizo: A person of mixed European and American Indian ancestry

Mosquitia: The Mosquito Coast in far northeast Honduras, characterized by swampy savannas, jungles, rivers, rapids, and marshy estuaries

personalismo: The Honduran regard for family and the individual

Private Export Processing Zones: Zones in which companies pay no taxes and no customs duties on imported materials or exported products. Companies also face no restrictions on the use of foreign exchange or repatriation of capital or profits.

punta: The traditional Garifuna dance-song

rentist: A foreign resident of independent means

Third Age (Tercera Edad): Legislation describing government benefits for Hondurans over age 65

Tourist Free Zone Law: a law that exempts tourist businesses from income tax on profits and sales tax on building materials. The law also allows for the duty-free import of materials and equipment, including motor vehicles, boats, and airplanes used in the tourist trade.

powder-keg countries. Presently it's the best location for your Technicolor dreams. But *why?*

Why Honduras?

"Honduras is an exquisite country of vast natural diversity, from the great pine forests of the central Olancho province, to the flat savannas of the eastern Mosquitia, to the endless acres of banana fields on the north coast, to some of the hemisphere's most spectacular coral reefs surrounding the Caribbean Bay Islands. By Central American standards, it is a peaceful and stable country with a working two-party system."[3] That's the impartial judgment of Clifford Krauss, who was for 20 years the *Wall Street Journal*'s Central American correspondent.

In that "diversity" lie its charm and wide-ranging appeal. It has two cultures: Caribbean and mestizo. It has islands of enchantment, sun-drenched coastlines, unpopulated golden beaches, wild rivers lashed with white waters, coves and bights that demand picnicking, and majestic mountains bristling with crests of pine. It has jungles teeming

James D. Gollin

The enchanting Bay Islands off the northern coast of Honduras

with exotic flora and fauna—the orchid and the nearly legendary quetzal, the jaguar and the tapir. It has cloud forests that present a panoply of birds, ruins and excavations, aboriginal settlements, colonial enclaves, crowded ports and bustling banana boats, oxen and burros, active and abandoned mines, fishing lakes and brooding marshes, and the marvelous mystery of the Maya in the town of Copán.

It has something for almost every taste. The second longest barrier reef in the world, the longest in the hemisphere—only Australia's can outmatch it—invites diving aficionados, delighted snorkelers, and yachtsmen. The uncrowded beaches that confront the reef offer every satisfaction that beaches anywhere can offer. Hikers, river rafters, bird-watchers, and adventurers respond to the rural parts of the mainland. Amateur and professional archaeologists, anthropologists, and sociologists find much to feed their intellectual appetites. And for the wearied traveler, the three biggest cities offer *some*—by no means all—of the comforts, sports, and pleasures a cosmopolite expects.

The retiree on a limited budget discovers that he can afford a lifestyle and even luxuries beyond his means in the States. The socially inclined need have no fear of solitude in a new and strange milieu because the expatriate residents of their new home serve as a ready-made support group, quick to aid them. Americans who speak Spanish find that an odd glamour attaches to their nationality and often gains them entry into distinguished Ladino social circles.

To the retiree and would-be resident who seeks a dream house, Honduras offers the chance of a plot of land and a house built *almost* to his specifications for perhaps—but we must be cautious here— half to a third of what a comparable location and building would cost in the States. And should you accept this assignment as retiree, you would enjoy a cost of living—providing that you buy mostly domestic goods and don't import much—between a third and a quarter of what it is at home.

And you need not give up all your vices either. Decent domestic liquors, beers, cigarettes, cigars, and pleasant South American wines seem almost shockingly low-priced, at least on the mainland. Furthermore, your comfort index may rise considerably. Domestic help that might seem extravagant at home is at your service, even if your retirement income is very moderate. Local workers who clean, cook, drive, launder, garden, guard, or serve as handymen cheerfully receive less than a fifth of stateside wages.

In many pleasant sections of Honduras, the Social Security income of the average retiree, prudently spent, will alone suffice for a comfortable life. A rough comparison of wages may help to make the point. On the Bay Islands, the country's most expensive area, a Honduran national who teaches in a public school is paid the equivalent of between $150 and $200 a month. If teachers can live decently on $200 a month, shouldn't a $600-a-month Social Security check serve you, once you know your way around?

On the mainland, that same teacher would rarely earn more than $100 monthly. Also on the mainland, a housekeeper will count herself lucky to receive room and board—beans and rice—and $60 a month in cash. At a higher point on the scale, a bird colonel in the

HELPFUL PUBLICATIONS

Local Papers
- *Coconut Telegraph* (Roatán)
- *Honduras Tips* (San Pedro Sula)
- *Utila Times* (Bay Islands)

Books
- *The Cruising Guide to the Honduras Bay Islands*, Westcott Cobe Publishers
- *Diving and Snorkeling Roatán and Honduras Bay Islands*, by Sharon Collins
- *Honduras: Adventures in Nature*, by James D. Gollin and Ron Mader, John Muir Publications
- *Honduras: The Owner's Manual*, International Living

Other Publications
- *International Living*
- *Honduras: Central American Adventure Magazine*

Honduran army can live well on a salary equivalent to about $900 a month. But pity the poor army private whose spending money amounts to six or seven dollars a month. These numbers don't prove so much that Honduras is "cheap" but instead show that the United States has grown so expensive.

To be sure, for the financial privilege, you will be leaving behind surroundings you know well. But you don't need to abandon your favorite armchair or that recliner bed you now enjoy. Resident retirees are granted a one-time-only privilege of bringing in all household goods free of duty. The family car is supposed to have the same immunity from customs, but there have been difficulties with this privilege, snarls that a determined Department of Tourism may have disentangled by the time you read this.

Finally, not one cent of your income from abroad—not your Social Security or investment income or the mattress money you have stashed—is subject to Honduran income tax. Those who have suffered IRS bites into their Social Security and dividends will lose no such blood to Honduran tax collectors.

To those retirees who contemplate not only residing but also investing and working in Honduras, opportunity is now flowering like a late-blooming water lily. In 1992 new laws laid down welcome mats in many directions, opening doors and avenues to foreign investment that previously had been shut or granted only restricted passage.

The labor pool is vast and as inexpensive as any in Central or South America. Industries that use the country's natural resources and are labor intensive should do well. Tax breaks and special incentives abound, and the government requires less paperwork than does the United States. In short, the country needs investors and investments and welcomes them.

Yes, Honduras offers a retirement garden of charm and beauty and ease, but not every person who plants himself here will flourish. Test the soil. See if the fruit of the tree is to your taste before putting down roots. The invariable rule when considering so large a move and so great a change is "Visit before you rent and rent before you buy."

A little rudimentary analysis of your needs and temperament is probably your best first step. If the first aspect you note in a stranger is skin pigmentation, stay away. If you shrink from visible poverty and shabbiness, no matter how cheerfully borne, you will be offended too often for comfort. If you are addicted to the cultural richness and variety of the great cities of the world, you will feel withdrawal pangs in most of Honduras. If you automatically equate third-world "backwardness" with laziness and incompetence, remember that a haughty mien, as the Bible warns, precedes a fall. Autocrats and slave-drivers need not apply. If you can't relax somewhat with a slightly carefree outlook, you'll paint yourself into a corner. If the word *mañana* makes you grind your teeth, it would be folly to invest your tomorrows anywhere in Central America, let alone Honduras.

Ours is a work-oriented culture. If your favorite mantra is "Time is money," you will need to recognize that time is the money you are going to be spending now and you should invest it wisely. You may have to reprogram yourself so that leisure occupies your main screen.

If, after extended visits, the country seems *simpático* and congru-

Belinda Linton and Bill Martin are among hundreds of Americans who call Honduras home

ent with your personality, consider applying for residency. For the price of a cottage in Long Island or Orange County you can build a near-castle set on a piece of paradise. Your heating budget alone in North Dakota would pay all expenses of comfortable living for a couple in Honduras.

Many retirees enjoy the privileges and security of residency without feeling the least bit confined by that status. They live in Honduras for much of the year while moving easily between other countries and returning to familiar scenes at their former home at will. Residency does not in any way affect your American citizenship, nor does applying for and receiving Honduran citizenship and a second passport impair it.

For that matter, you can buy a house and land without bothering to seek residency approval. You can live in Honduras on a visa (which must be renewed monthly with a ten-lempira stamp at the bank), but every six months the present law requires you to leave the country for three days, re-entering on a new visa. A few expatriates I've met follow this pattern, although two of them confide that they go out for only one day, since the three-day absence is not usually enforced.

Honduras is democratic, politically stable, and relatively free of violent crime. It is accessible—two hours flying time from Miami. It has siren beauty and charm. And it has three more strong assets: its temperate climate, its low cost of living, and, above all, its people.

---

1. Peter Dickinson, *Travel and Retirement Edens Abroad*, second edition (New York: Scott, Foresman and Company, 1989), 5. The author, a pioneering expert on retirement for many years, does not discuss Honduras in this book.

2. Shelley Emling, *Your Guide to Retiring to Mexico, Costa Rica and Beyond*, (Garden City, N.Y.: Avery Publishing Group, 1996), 135, 146. This book does not include Honduras but does deal with Guatemala and Ecuador.

3. Clifford Krauss, *Inside Central America*, (New York: Summit Books, 1991), 180.

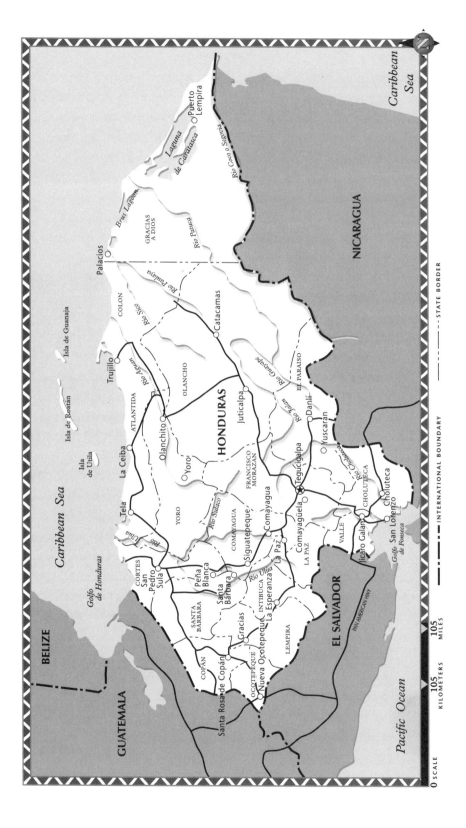

2

▼▲▼

Overview of a Potential Paradise

H onduras is the second largest country in Central America. Only Nicaragua is larger. Its skewed triangle of 43,644 square miles slightly exceeds the area of Tennessee and fits midway in size between Louisiana and Pennsylvania. It runs from 16 degrees north of the equator down to 13—about 500 miles north of the equator. Crosswise it stretches from about 83 degrees west—a straight shot down from Tampa, Florida—to about 89½ degrees west, where it looks up at New Orleans.

The Caribbean coast forms the 457-mile northern boundary. North of the coast lie the Bay Islands, increasingly a tourist mecca, surrounded by a virtual archipelago of islets. The islands, now Honduran, were once part of a British crown colony.

The diagonal southeastern leg of the triangle is the 573-mile border with Nicaragua. It follows the Río Coco for almost half its length, then continues southwestward through mountainous terrain to a 90-mile strip along the Gulf of Fonseca on the Pacific. Nicaragua and El Salvador own parts of the gulf along with Honduras.

Turning upward northwest is the 231-mile western border shared with El Salvador, the subject of centuries of dispute, only recently settled in 1993. Above that is the 159-mile border with Guatemala.

Honduras is called "the Tibet of Central America" for its mountainous landscape. A third of the country is forest and woodlands, and only a little less is given over to pastures and meadows. Barely one-seventh is arable, yielding coffee, tobacco, cacao, palm oil, sorghum, wheat, beans, corn, and other vegetables, and, of course, bananas, pineapples, and other fruits. The alluvial plains on the Caribbean are only a few miles wide at Trujillo but elsewhere stretch into river valleys, the largest of which holds Puerto Cortés, the chief shipping port, and San Pedro Sula, the commercial center. On the east are the lowlands of the Mosquitia, the "Mosquito Coast," a waterlogged savanna.

One long high-altitude valley runs from the area near San Pedro through Comayagua, passing Honduras's only natural lake. Lake

James D. Gollin

Honduras touches the Pacific for 90 miles along the Gulf of Fonseca.

Yojoa, 14 miles long and 125 feet deep, is beautifully clear on its diet of underground springs. The valley continues southward until it encounters the border of El Salvador, affording relatively easy transportation across the isthmus to the shore of the Gulf of Fonseca, the site of cotton and rice fields and cattle ranches.

Climate

Naturally you are concerned about heat and weather. The very word *tropics* may conjure up a picture of residents melting down to a puddle in the roadway. And yes, the Caribbean lowlands have a tropical wet climate with consistently high temperatures and humidity. So don't expect those few things you rinsed out last night to be dry this morning. The trade winds encountering the Nombre de Dios Mountains that rise suddenly from the northern coastal region tend to dump their moisture frequently. Tela and La Ceiba on the North Coast get about three times as much rain annually as Houston or New York, but dry out considerably between November and May.

Daytime average temperatures range from 84 to 91°F. The Pacific lowlands around the gulf experience similar heat but, when the prevailing winds change in November, the lowlands have a distinct dry season that runs through April—the hottest month but surprisingly comfortable.

The Bay Islands, farther away from the mountains, get less rain, most of it from Columbus Day to New Year's, and are driest in spring. Surrounded by the sea, the islands rarely top 84°F and drop to an average of 78°F in January.

In all tropical countries how hot you are depends on how high you are. In the central highlands at 1,000 meters (about 3,100 feet) daytime averages run about 81°F and dip to about 60°F at night. The land between 1,000 and 2,000 meters (about 6,200 feet) is called "temperate," with 75°F more common than 85°F. Tegucigalpa, at 3,200 feet, just edges into the temperate zone, with cool nights and warm, but rarely excessively hot, days. Above 2,000 meters the region is called "cold" because frost sometimes occurs at night, although 80°F days are not uncommon.

It is probably more accurate to speak of Honduran weathers than weather. Even on the rainiest days there is almost always an interval of sun, and you can usually find ideal weather some place in Honduras at any time of the year. It is safe to say that when the States are at their coldest and most unfriendly, Honduras is enjoying pleasant weather. Your Honduran wardrobe should accent summer clothing but should not omit rainwear and a light sweater, jacket, or sports coat for cool nights.

Except for a disastrous quake in 1974, Honduras is less bothered by serious earthquakes than its immediate neighbors and is free of the active volcanoes that trouble them as well. (Nicaragua has more active volcanoes per square mile than any other country in the world.) On the Bay Islands people boast that only one person has died there from a hurricane: a man who fell off a roof he was patching the next day.

Population

Since the last reliable estimate of the population was 5.1 million in 1991 and the growth rate was approximated at 3.1 percent, the present total population must be about 6 million. Per square mile, Honduras has less than a quarter of the density of crowded El Salvador.

But the search for employment has drawn many people out of the mountainous southwest and into the cities. Contrast the least populated *departamento* (like a state), Gracias a Dios, with about seven people per square mile, with the bustling department of Cortés, with 487 people per square mile. San Pedro Sula and Tegucigalpa are projected to account for one-fourth of the total population of Honduras by the year 2000. Even now, in those cities, few houses are for sale and rentals are scarce and becoming expensive.

Honduran society is rural and poor. More than half of its people dwell in the countryside at a bare subsistence level. Inadequate nutrition, housing, and poor sanitation facilities in the countryside have kept life expectancy low. Males average just under 66 years, females on average live five years more. The four percent of the population who manage to reach 65 have traditionally been called "ancient."

Education is free and mandatory for children between ages 7 and 15, and compliance has improved markedly in the last decade. In 1993 Unesco estimated that nearly 90 percent of eligible children were attending primary school. However, because of widespread poverty, the law allows children to leave school for work with the consent of both parents. Consequently, Unesco presently classifies 27 percent of Hondurans as illiterate, a dismaying tally but better than the scores of El Salvador and Nicaragua.

The official language of mainland Honduras is Spanish, although English is spoken widely in commercial circles, especially in the north. If the language is a problem for you, the "Se Habla Español" (Spanish Spoken) chapter discusses the matter at length. You may be reassured to know that on the Bay Islands, English is the official language. Ethnically, nine out of ten residents are *mestizos*, a mixture of white and Amerindian. A demographic discussion of the population occupies the end of "The People" chapter.

Religion

Religion has always played a strong role in Honduras. Catholicism claims about 93.5 percent membership, although many Hondurans have only a nominal or social allegiance to the church.

The Catholic Church has occupied a privileged position in Honduras since the Spanish occupation. Church schools receive government subsidies, and religious instruction is part of the public school curriculum. Not surprisingly, in view of the church's influence, children in public schools wear uniforms: boys in white shirts and dark blue slacks, girls in white blouses and blue or black skirts. They make a charming picture spilling out at recess, but the efforts of the poorest families to patch together a uniform out of odd remnants are sometimes apparent.

With the Second Vatican Council and its message that church members should be active agents of social change, the church, although traditionally conservative, began to press for social reform. But as the polarization of the Cold War intensified, reform became more identified with radicalism. In the 1980s some priests were accused of being communists, and activism eased almost to a halt. With the fall of the Berlin Wall, calls for change can again be heard in Honduras.

In the older, more established circles of elite society, the strictures of the Catholic Church bind more tightly. While members of an unhappy marriage may find solace elsewhere without being considered beyond the pale, seeking a divorce, especially if the woman breaks the union, is likely to place the divorcee in Coventry. And that same woman may find doorways to suitable employment closed to her.

Among the poor, Catholicism is less visible. Church weddings are avoided as too expensive, and church-sanctioned annulments require too great an investment of time and money. Therefore most marriages in Honduras are civil ceremonies. "Free" unions are also common. An errant male who fathers children outside the home is condemned only if he fails to support them.

Religious freedom is constitutionally guaranteed, and in recent years evangelical Protestant groups have made many converts.

James D. Gollin

Colonial-era churches, such as this one in Gracias, dot Honduran towns and cities.

Protestantism is especially strong on the Bay Islands because of their English heritage. Regardless of individual denominations, Protestants are usually called "evangelicals": perhaps because their services in Honduras are usually more activist and missionary than they are in the States. The largest numbers are found in Methodist, Church of God, Seventh-Day Adventist, and Assemblies of God congregations. They sponsor social service programs in many communities. Their political influence has generally been conservative.

In spite of this new pluralism, the Catholic holy days are holidays, and the nation at least pays lip service to Catholic customs. This will concern you when making appointments in Honduras. To even the least religious Honduran, all holidays are holy in the sense that no work is to be considered.

Products

Bananas and coffee accounted for 50 percent of the value of Honduran exports in 1992, with sales of about $435 million. Chiquita Brands and Dole have bought out most of the independent banana producers. Coffee in Honduras is grown by many small producers. As a result, the growers of that crop have not aroused the enmity of other farmers the way the large coffee plantations did in El Salvador. Still, coffee crop productivity serves as an example of poor agricultural management. Honduras's yield per acre is about half that of Costa Rica's.

During the Nicaraguan war, sugar became a boom crop in Honduras. But in 1993, when Nicaragua had its sugar quota to the States restored, sugar income dropped. And while tobacco is a burgeoning crop, the decline of world prices and drought have reduced the profitability of beef exports.

Honduras's tiny manufacturing sector, one of the smallest in Central America, mostly in clothing, employs only about 10 percent of the workforce. The natural resources are timber, gold, silver, copper, lead, zinc, iron ore, antimony, coal, fish, and, in the Mosquitia, rubber trees, mahogany, and other hardwoods.

Erosion and loss of soil fertility due to deforestation and traditional slash-and-burn farming are serious problems in Honduras, as is water pollution caused by chemical runoff from mining. The loss of indigenous biodiversity and the degradation of marine resources are also arousing concern. In 1993, with the establishment of the Environmental Ministry, the Honduran government began to face its environmental problems and since then has been developing comprehensive policies to deal with them sensitively yet realistically.

Rights and Freedoms

Freedoms of speech, press, and religion are guaranteed by the Honduran constitution. These freedoms are genuine and generally respected. The relative openness of Honduran politics and the degree of legitimacy given to working-class demands have resulted in a system in which organizations representing the lower sectors of society can be highly organized, even militant, without calling for the overthrow of the system itself. According to some analysts, Honduras has achieved a level of political organization on the part of labor unions and peasant organizations that remains unparalleled in most of Central America.

Despite occasional lapses, the mostly conservative press in Honduras is free of deliberate deceit and has helped to create a democratic culture and an atmosphere of open criticism of authorities. Radio is at least as important as the written word, and it is the primary source of information for the third of the population tagged as illiterate or semiliterate. Local television—perhaps a dozen outlets—is supplemented by cable receiving U.S. and Mexican programs, but it carries less weight than radio because its cost is beyond the reach of most.

Adding to the gamut of freely voiced opinion is the National Autonomous University of Honduras (UNAH) with its 30,000 students usually expressing a liberal viewpoint. Honduras also has three small private universities, but these have not yet been able to approach the prestige of the senior institution.

Government

A democratic republic, Honduras is a union of 18 departments. Every Honduran citizen 18 and over is eligible to vote for the president and deputies of the National Congress, the legislative body. He or she votes for the president and deputies on the slate of the party preferred.

The two political parties with the largest followings are the Liberal Party (PL) and the National Party (PNP). Although the National Party was formerly named the Conservative Party and describes itself as the more conservative, ideologically the two parties are not very far apart. A third party, the Christian Democratic Party (PDC), has never been a strong contender. In one election, 81 percent of eligible voters went to the polls, a comparison that rebukes American apathy.

The president, who must be a native-born citizen, is elected by a simple majority for one four-year term. He is prohibited from reelection. He is general commander of the armed forces, directing them through their commander in chief. He is the director of all policy, foreign and domestic, except for security matters, which remain under the military. With his cabinet he is responsible for drawing up plans of national development and submitting them to the National Congress. He appoints all 14 ministers of his cabinet, giving each charge of a ministry.

James D. Gollin

Honduras welcomes industries, such as this cigar factory, and encourages foreign investment.

The ministries number 13 at this writing, with new ones in the process of creation. Besides such obvious ones as Foreign Affairs, Finance, and Education, those of special interest to the expatriate visitor or retiree are the ministries of Industry and Trade, Public Works, Transportation and Housing, and Culture, Arts, and Sports.

The work of the ministries is supplemented by standing decentralized agencies like the Social Security Institute, the National Council of Social Welfare, and the National Electrical Energy

Enterprise. In addition, the president creates commissions. Three very active ones are commissions on Modernization of the State, Institutional Reform, and Government Corruption.

The National Congress is a unicameral body with the national parties represented in proportion to their electoral support. Although individual deputies may initiate bills, in practice most are introduced by the executive branch. A bill must be debated three days before a vote. If the bill is passed, unless vetoed by the president within ten days, it becomes law as soon as it is published in the *Gaceta Judicial*, the government's official journal. A two-thirds majority is required to override a veto.

Deputies are elected for four-year terms at the same time as the president. These 128 representatives not only legislate and control the budget and taxation but also elect many government officials.

You will immediately recognize this body's resemblance to the U.S. House of Representatives, but there is a major difference. Although in theory the deputies represent one or another of the 18 *departamentos*, because of an odd feature in the electoral law, they have had no direct accountability to the electorate. The unitary ballot joins a party's presidential candidate with that party's list of congressional candidates. Until 1997, the voter could not split his vote. (Now there are separate ballots for deputies and for mayor.)

> "In one election, 81 pecent of eligible voters went to the polls, a comparison that rebukes American apathy."

Thus the deputies are more bound by party loyalty than by the needs of their constituents. Representation is often further diluted by substitution: the elected deputies, often wealthy party favorites, are at times too busy to attend congress and send their alternate delegates *(suplentes)* to sit for them.

Political patronage has led to a bloated bureaucracy. In 1990 this tiny country had over 70,000 government employees. Recent presidents have tried cutbacks, but rumor has it that the total plays like an accordion.

The judicial branch consists of a Supreme Court of Justice, courts of appeal, courts of first instance (trial courts), and justices of the peace. This branch has been a frequent target of severe criticism. The executive controls the selection of judges, and patronage weighs more than competence in the process. It is hardly surprising that John Dupuis, editor of the valuable *Honduras Tips*, identifies the country's chief political problem as the "total spoils system" followed by either of the victorious major parties.

The president also appoints the governors of the 18 departments. These are divided into 291 *municipios* (much like our county governments), administered by elected corporations consisting of a mayor and a council. Further subdivisions are villages and hamlets or, in large cities, colonies and neighborhoods (the familiar *barrios*).

As you read Central American history and consider life in those countries, you cannot help being concerned about the possibility of an army takeover of the country you might choose. A sign of Honduras's increasingly wary attitude toward its military appears in a recent amendment to Article 2 of the 1982 constitution. Article 2 states, as behooves a republic, that sovereignty originates in the people. Seemingly inspired by the historical record of innumerable military coups, the amendment brands supplanting popular sovereignty and usurping power as "crimes of treason."

In the fifth title (chapter) of the document, the armed forces are described as an "apolitical, obedient, and non-deliberative institution," a profile perhaps more wishful than realistic. In practice, the military continues to exercise significant influence, but it does seem to have forsworn direct intervention. The World Bank and other international lending institutions have pressured Honduras to restrict the role of the military.

In general, cronyism and corruption still impede the efficiency of government, but political and social reform seem to be making headway. Honduras may yet emerge, not as a banana republic, but as a republic not only of and by the people but *for* the people.

3

▼▲▼▲▼▲▼▲▼▲▼▲▼▲▼▲▼▲▼▲▼▲▼▲▼▲▼▲▼▲▼▲▼▲▼▲▼▲▼

History of Honduras

A hunter-gatherer culture lived in western and central Honduras at least 10,000 years ago. Gradually they began to farm and make pottery. Pottery shards date to 2000 B.C. Recent excavations along the Talgua River reveal a fairly advanced trading civilization, with elaborate funerary customs, dating from about 1400 B.C. The Mayas made their presence felt in the region from about 1000 B.C. They built temples and other ceremonial structures.

Between A.D. 300 and 600, the Mayas built a great city at Copán, mastered mathematics, including the concept of zero, made astronomical discoveries, and then fell into a strange decline, halting all progress there by 850. They migrated to the Yucatán and, as a dominant culture, vanished before Columbus arrived.

Spain Arrives

In 1502, on his fourth and last voyage, Christopher Columbus landed briefly on the second largest of the Bay Islands, Guanaja, which he named the Island of Pines, and made a brief landfall on the coast of what he called Honduras (meaning "depths" in Spanish). His brother Bartholomew celebrated the first mainland Catholic mass at what is now Trujillo.

Spain ignored seemingly unprofitable Honduras until 1524, when five rival expeditions invaded, warring first with the indigenous tribes and then with one another. Hernán Cortéz made a brief appearance, restored order, established a headquarters at Trujillo, and subdued the local chiefs. Colonial governors who followed began cities in San Pedro Sula and Comayagua but inspired resentment among the indigenous population—already in decline from imported smallpox and venereal disease. Harsh colonial policies included exportation of natives as slaves to the Caribbean Islands.

In the 1530s the discovery of gold created a gold rush at a mining center called Gracias. New settlers pressed native people to work in the mines. This forced labor provoked a major uprising in 1537, led by a charismatic young Lenca chieftain named Lempira. He fortified a hilltop, and for two years his army of about 30,000 Lencas, joined by neighboring Indian nations, fought a large Spanish force with Mexican allies to a standstill.

Treachery won the day. Under a flag of truce and promise of negotiation, a Spanish delegation was admitted to the fort, whereupon they murdered Lempira and overpowered the garrison. The heroic chief is memorialized in the name given to Honduran currency, and his portrait graces the one-lempira note.

The key economic activity of sixteenth-century Honduras was the mining of gold and silver, which gradually shifted eastward to Comayagua. It was mining that gave birth to the Ladino (*Latin* plus *Indian*) culture, the mestizo culture that differentiates Honduras from its neighbors. The Amerindians pressed to labor in the mines came from different villages and spoke different languages. Forced to communicate with each other and with their masters, they adopted the colonial language. Intermarriage followed, and the distinctive Ladino culture was born.

The shrinkage of the native population and the discovery of more gold near the coast prompted the Spanish masters to an ignoble trade. In the next few years they imported an estimated two thousand African slaves, a depravity without sustained profit, for mining soon dwindled. A silver strike led to the founding of Tegucigalpa—"silver hill" in the local dialect—but that flurry also died, and Honduras declined into an economic backwater, a subordinate of Guatemala.

The next century proved no more prosperous. Colonial government became an almost profitless task, with only a few Spanish families in Tegucigalpa or even in the then capital Comayagua. Royal taxes were diverted by corrupt mining outfits, and extensive smuggling on the coast hampered what little export there was.

When the Bourbon Dynasty replaced the Hapsburgs on the throne of Spain with Philip V in 1700, the new rulers attempted some reforms but found themselves faced with a more vexing problem in the English. English corsairs had long attacked the Caribbean coast. In 1643 they destroyed Trujillo, which had served as Honduras's major port.

For more than a century, the English, aided by the Sambo and Miskito tribes of mixed African and Native American ancestry, forcibly planted colonies on the coast and especially in the Bay Islands, trading in Honduran hardwoods and pitch.

The Spaniards retaliated and, in 1786, the Anglo-Spanish Convention recognized Spanish sovereignty over the coast. But the British had a protectorate over Belize, then called British Honduras, and continued to exercise control to the south.

It was too late for Spain. In 1808 Napoleon sent the Spanish king into exile and put a Bonaparte on the throne. Revolts in Madrid and elsewhere in Spain were echoed by uprisings in Latin America, fired further by an attempt to increase taxes to aid the exiled king.

Independence

On September 15, 1821, the five "provinces of Central America"—Guatemala, Honduras, El Salvador, Nicaragua, and Panama—declared independence. In Honduras, Tegucigalpa urged the creation of a unified Central American state, while resentful Comayagua favored union with the Empire of Mexico.

Mexico briefly accepted the allegiance of its southern neighbors, but in 1823 the empire was overthrown and Mexico became a republic. A new federation, the United Provinces of Central America, in which Comayagua was represented but Tegucigalpa had no seat, declared independence from Mexico as well. Its greatest achievement was the emancipation of all slaves, anticipating Britain's abolition of slavery by a decade.

The hostile rivalry between Honduras's two major cities was paralleled by a political split throughout the isthmus between conservative and liberal factions. According to *Honduras: A Country Study*, "The conservatives favored a more centralized government, a proclerical policy, including a church monopoly over education, and a more aristocratic form of government based on traditional Spanish values. The liberals wanted greater local autonomy and a restricted role for the church, as well as political and economic development as in the United States and parts of Western Europe. The conservatives favored keeping native people in their traditional subservient position, while the liberals aimed at eventually eliminating indigenous society by incorporating it

Young drummers join an Independence Day (September 15) parade.

James D. Gollin

into the national, Hispanic culture."[1] These factions inevitably clashed, not only in legislative chambers but also at sword points.

In 1830 a Honduran liberal, General Francisco Morazán (the George Washington of Central America), having repelled an invasion of Honduras and unseated the Guatemalan power center, won the presidency of the federation. For a decade he fought valiantly to keep the new union intact, but in 1838 the Central American Congress removed him from office and dissolved the union, proclaiming the freedom of the five individual states as "sovereign, free, and independent political bodies." In 1842 Morazán, still trying to preserve the ideal of unity, was shot in Costa Rica.

Clifford Krauss provides an acerb, ironic footnote to the meteoric career of this Honduran national hero: "In Tegucigalpa the capital's most patriotic monument, the equestrian statue of Honduran liberator Francisco Morazán, is an insult. Though Morazán's name is inscribed on the base, it is really the likeness of Marshal Michel Ney of France that graces Honduras' central plaza. As legend has it, the Honduran board responsible for commissioning the monument stole so much money it was obliged to acquire the French statue on the cheap to avert a public scandal. . . . A French Morazán [had to] do." [2]

Finally, on November 15, 1838, Honduras declared its independence and adopted a new constitution, the first of many. But this gesture of independence was weak. With Honduras in chaos, the British took advantage by reestablishing control of the Bay Islands. For the remainder of the century, the British, as well as Honduras's neighbors, Guatemala, Nicaragua, and El Salvador, constantly interfered in the country's internal politics.

A dramatic interruption of local troubles arrived with William Walker, an American doctor, lawyer, journalist, and soldier of fortune. Having earlier seized Nicaragua and proclaimed himself governor, receiving Washington's recognition, he had been driven back to the States. In 1859, when the British agreed to withdraw from their "crown colony" in the Bay Islands, Walker and his "filibusterer" followers, counting on islanders' resentment of the new mainland rule, returned, hoping to use the islands as a base for seizure of Honduras. Although he managed to capture Trujillo, he

Honduras's Great Mystery

The most impressive sight in all Honduras is surely the ruins at Copán, a legacy in stone of a sophisticated and mysterious people. Copán is a jewel in a limestone necklace of lost Mayan cities extending north through Guatemala, Belize, and the Yucatán in Mexico. Not the largest of the cities—Tikál on Guatemala was four times its size and Chichén Itzá in the Yucatán has more towering structures—Copán surpasses them all in the intricacy of its artwork, the deep carving of its trachyte monuments, and the splendor of its ornamentation.

In the last 20 years much of the mystery has given way before the industry of scholars. The written language of the stone inscriptions has been deciphered and almost all of the mute cartouches have been interpreted. Today we know a lot about the history, achievements, and festivals of these stargazers and calendar-keepers of more than a millennium ago. We know of their dynastic rivalries, fierce warfare, and obsession with bloodletting. We know of their passion for art, their appreciation of the intellect, their cyclic view of time and creation, and their incursions into the otherworld of the supernatural.

One great mystery, however, still remains and perhaps always will. What happened to them? For at least six centuries they lived in pride and power, with a shared culture and language extending across a thousand miles of separate cities, and then, sometime in the late 800s, this great civilization collapsed and disappeared, their cities buried in mounds under jungle vegetation and the dust of centuries.

When you view the incredible masses of shaped and carved stones you are confronted by another mystery of the Maya: How did they do it? How did they haul and raise such tonnage? For all its knowledge, this great civilization lacked two important tools of transport and construction: They never invented the wheel and they never domesticated animals, except dogs, which they used for hunting and food.

Add to this the fact that no metal tools have been traced further back than A.D. 900: The monumental work done by the Mayas was accomplished with fired hardwood, hard stone tools, and obsidian knives.

James Gollin

met determined opposition and surrendered to the British with assurance of safe conduct. The British, however, hoping to collect some old Honduran debts, reneged and turned him over to the Honduran authorities, who executed him by firing squad in 1860. His fenced-in grave lies in Trujillo's cemetery.

The political events of the next generation suggest improbable comic opera plots. The president who saw to Walker's demise was murdered in 1862 by his own honor guard. The following decade saw two more new constitutions adopted and the presidency change hands almost 20 times. Term limits meant nothing. One general, appearing and disappearing like the Cheshire cat, served as president or dictator 11 times.

"Many hands make light work" is an old saw, but for most of Honduras's history, too many hands at the helm have made for little progress. In the nearly 160 years since its independence, Honduras has had some 16 different constitutions, more than 100 presidents, caudillos, and military heads of state, and about 300 changes of government, power grabs, and internal rebellions.

The weakness of its political development left the country primitive in its economy, backward in its infrastructure, uninviting to international trade, and susceptible to frequent manipulation by outside interests. Yet that same instability, that lack of any long-dominant dictator or junta, has meant that the structures and machinery of oppression and exploitation never formed, and the Honduran people, despite their poverty, escaped the virtual enslavement that oligarchies of landowners demanded from time to time in Guatemala and El Salvador.

Order was restored and some basic reforms, including separation of church and state, were implemented under President Marco Aurelio Soto. During his time in office, the capital was moved from Comayagua to Tegucigalpa because, it is rumored, the society of the former city had snubbed Soto's Guatemalan Indian wife. His resignation in 1883 was caused not by internal dissatisfaction but by the disfavor of the Guatemalan caudillo General Barrios.

Yet the same outside influence helped the overthrow of the military dictatorship that followed and enabled the ascension,

TIME LINE

1502 Columbus arrives on Guanaja

1524 Hernán Cortéz restores order with warring indigenous tribes; establishes Trujillo

1530 Gold discovered

1539 Murder of Lempira; collapse of Amerindian resistance to Spain

1643 Trujillo destroyed

1821 The five provinces—Guatemala, El Salvador, Honduras, Nicaragua, and Panama—declare their independence

1823 Mexico becomes a republic

1830 General Francisco Morazán becomes president of the Central American federation

1838 Honduras declares its independence

1842 Morazán is assassinated

1899 First banana shipment from Honduras to New Orleans

1923 Central American states meet in Washington, D.C., to adopt a general Treaty of Peace and Amity

1932 General Tibercio Carías Andino elected president

1963 Villeda Morales seeks political exile; Colonel López Arellano comes to power

1969 Soccer War

1974 Hurricane Fifi causes widespread devastation in Honduras

1980 Peace agreement and settlement of border claims with El Salvador

1982 Roberto Suazo Córdova takes office; American military aid increases tenfold

1985 José Azcona Hoyo elected president

1987 Outside aid to insurgent forces comes to a stop

1993 Central American Free Trade Zone established

1998 Carlos Flores Facusse dons the official sash as the fifth freely elected president in succession under another constitution, of Policarpo Bonilla, whose active government revised administrative codes, encouraged investment, and tried to resolve the boundary dispute with Nicaragua. At the end of his term in 1899, a new president succeeded to office legally and constitutionally for the first time in decades.

Yes, We Have Bananas

The year 1899 marks another transition. The Vaccaro brothers of New Orleans, founders of what was to become the Standard Fruit Company, shipped their first boatload of bananas from Honduras to New Orleans. Shortly, banana companies—United, Cuyamel, and others—flourished amid a shower of privileges from a grateful government.

One cynical entrepreneur, Sam "the banana man" Zemurray, commenting on the sorry political conditions, noted that a mule cost more than a congressman.[3] He later overthrew a president by a show of a surplus gunboat and American machine guns.

Taxes on banana exports became the lifeblood of the Honduran economy. In short order, Honduras became the world's leading exporter of bananas—accounting for one-third of the world's supply—and the quintessential banana republic, a belittling sobriquet that it is only now beginning to shuck.

The banana companies proved a mixed blessing for a generation. Through abundant local employment, worker welfare systems, health clinics, and company stores, they became more important to hundreds of thousands of Hondurans than their own government. Wages were hardly generous, but they were reliable and at least on a par with other export industries of the time.

On the other hand, the company railroads did little for the country's infrastructure because the tracks ran only from fields to ports. In addition, repressive working conditions, barracks-style accommodations, and, later, military intervention and goon squad strikebreakers bred labor unrest. Major strikes started in 1917, and in 1920 a general strike hit the Caribbean coast. U.S. warships steamed south, and the Honduran government began arresting strike leaders. When Standard Fruit offered a new wage equal to $1.75 a day, the strike collapsed.

American pressure had been growing, both to protect American banana interests by landing marines in Puerto Cortés in 1907 and to cut European influence in Central America by means of dollar diplomacy. Honduras contributed considerably to American concern over Central American instability. Invasions by its neighbors, internal uprisings and coups, and power plays by banana companies had made the Honduran presidency a game of musical chairs.

In 1923 a general meeting of the Central American states in Washington adopted a General Treaty of Peace and Amity. The treaty denied recognition to any revolutionary leader who had been in power six months before or after an uprising unless a free election had been held in the interim.

For all that, it wasn't until the 1932 election of General Tibercio Carías Andino that there was any continuity of leadership. His 16 years of presidency, made possible by a series of constitutional amendments, was the longest period of continuous rule by any individual in Honduran history. He faced two great problems: First, the Great Depression brought a collapse of prices, wage cuts, layoffs, labor disturbances, and increased indebtedness. Second, local epidemics of a fungus called Panama disease, along with leaf blight, devastated banana production. Large fields were abandoned, and thousands lost jobs. Although a remedy for the disease was found in five years, Honduras had by then lost its preeminence in the banana trade.

Carías, both a military and a Renaissance man, probably saved the nation fiscally, making regular payments on Honduran debt, even clearing two small loans completely. He extended the badly needed roadways and modernized the army, founding the Military Aviation School in 1934. He made concessions to the rival Liberal Party but outlawed the Communist Party. He opposed strikes, earning the gratitude of the banana companies. He handpicked a Constituent Assembly in 1936 to rewrite the 1924 constitution, which no one had complained about, and through its changes remained in office until 1949.

His successor, Juan Manuel Galvez, continued the road building, supported coffee production, and paid off much of the country's external debt. But he took some independent steps. He put money into education, supported passage of the first income tax, restored much freedom to the press, and allowed organizing by the liberals and labor organizations. In his term, congress legislated the eight-hour workday and regulated the employment of women and children.

At the end of his term Galvez took a giant step backward from Honduran self-reliance, prompted by a crippling series of strikes involving some 30,000 workers. Attributing the labor unrest to leftist Guatemalan agitators, he entered into a military assistance program to aid the United States in toppling the elected left-leaning Guatemalan President Colonel Jacob Arbenz Guzmán. Arbenz had expropriated United Fruit lands in Guatemala.

Honduras, attributing to Guatemalan infection the internal strikes braking the banana business to a virtual standstill and rapidly spreading to other industries, joined in a military agreement with the United States. As a consequence, Honduras then became a passageway for the covert shipping of arms to Guatemalan rebels and provided a base for CIA-backed forces. After Arbenz fled into exile, the Honduran strikes were settled, with some benefits conceded to the workers but more to

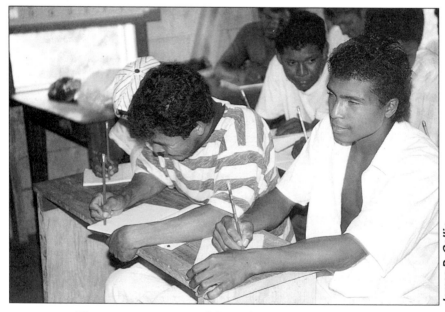

These young men are training to become lobster divers.

the fruit companies. Nevertheless, labor had begun to acquire a recognized voice and the following year adopted a legislated labor code.

Two constitutions and one coup later, the administration of Villeda Morales finally paved a highway between Tegucigalpa and the Caribbean coast. His administration built schools, passed a new labor code, began agrarian reform, established a social security system, sponsored a peasant union, and approved a partial resettlement of idle land.

Though elected for a six-year term, Villeda Morales was flown into exile in the last year of his presidency in 1963. A military coup empowered Colonel López Arellano, who promulgated yet another constitution, bonded with the National Party, and got himself elected president a year later. It was during his term that relations with San Salvador deteriorated into open conflict.

The Soccer War

Over a two-year period, about 300,000 undocumented Salvadoran immigrants, pushed out of their overcrowded country by its coffee-plantation economy, edged over the disputed boundary onto Honduran soil. In 1969 a Honduran land reform law left many of those Salvadoran families homeless and denied them the right to own land of their own. Official expulsions sparked open hostility, which came to a head in June 1969 in El Salvador during a World Cup match. Fighting broke out and the Honduran flag and national anthem were insulted.

In Honduras, violence against Salvadoran residents caused thousands to flee amid inflammatory press broadsides from both countries. A four-day war broke out. The Salvadoran army invaded, driving back the ill-trained Honduran foot soldiers about five miles and threatening Honduran islands in the Gulf of Fonseca. The Honduran air force evened the scales by destroying much of the small Salvadoran air force and bombing El Salvador's refinery, slowing their army's fuel supply.

After four days of bitter fighting, during which two thousand people were killed and thousands made homeless, the Organization of American States brokered a cease-fire and imposed a demilitarized zone along the border. Both countries suffered economically, and Honduras dropped out of the Central American Common Market. Real peace and settlement of border claims had to wait until 1980.

The war, however, engendered a spirit of nationalism among the citizens of Honduras, while the army lost support because of its lackluster showing. Calls for reform mounted, organizations of business, labor, and peasantry multiplied, and 20,000 peasants staged a hunger march on Tegucigalpa.

Then, in September 1974, the major natural disaster in modern Honduran history struck. Hurricane Fifi took 10,000 lives and a large part of the banana industry. A storm of scandal ensued, with allegations that the vital export tax on bananas had been repealed because United Brands (the new name of United Fruit) had bribed the government. Recoiling from this "Bananagate," the military forced López Arellano, its appointee president, out of office, and in Manhattan the president of United Brands committed suicide.

Dictatorship, corruption, and military repression followed, until in 1978 a three-man junta cleared the decks and promised a return to civilian rule, a pledge confirmed by strong signals from Washington, worried about leftist insurgencies in Central America.

In 1980 the first elections to the General Assembly drew more than one million Honduran voters. The new congress drafted a new constitution and electoral laws that enabled Roberto Suazo Córdova to take office in 1982, ending nearly a decade of military presidencies. A country doctor, he soon found himself in an international hot seat.

The Contra Presence

When the Sandanistas (FSLN) overthrew Anastasio Somoza in July 1979, Washington decided to step in. The U.S. government determined to shore up Honduras as a politically secure base against both the Sandanistas in Nicaragua and growing Marxist activities in El Salvador. Between 1980 and 1990, the United States gave more than

$1.2 billion in economic and subsistance aid. General Alvarez Martinez won control of the military and proclaimed Honduras an enemy of Nicaragua. He is reported to have "disappeared" many Honduran rebels supported by the Sandanistas.

Rule in Honduras became a three-legged stool. Alvarez formulated national security, Suazo went along with that policy in return for military support for his domestic acts, and U.S. assistance supplied the third leg. American military aid increased almost tenfold to more than $31 million in 1982.

Alvarez is said to have aided in the formation of the Nicaraguan resistance (the *contra-revolucionarios*, from which the name Contras emerged). Their bases and training camps, set up with CIA help, displaced many native Hondurans and acted as springboards for raids and clashes along the border with Nicaragua.

In those same years, the CIA united Honduran soldiers with Salvadoran troops fighting that country's leftist guerrillas. American Special Forces set up training camps. Fearing that the United States intended a direct strike at Nicaragua and that Alvarez was too ambitious and too subservient to the "gringos," a clique of senior Honduras officers exiled Alvarez and replaced him with General Walter Lopez, an air force hero of the Soccer War.

Lopez opposed having the Contras, a foreign military force of about 15,000 armed men and equal in size to Honduras's own army, on Honduran territory. He feared that Honduras might become another Lebanon. But with over $1 billion coming from the American pump in the 1980s, official Honduran policy remained ambivalent. In the end, the 60 percent of that money that took the form of politically motivated cash transfers did little good to Honduras because of the decade-long imbroglio and corruption among military and government officials. Economic development lagged because easy outside money postponed economic reform, investment declined, and the national debt mushroomed. By the mid-1980s the Boland Amendment and a changed American outlook restricted the flow of funds and arms.

The International Monetary Fund (IMF) demanded that Suazo implement an austerity program. "Produce more, export more, consume less, and spend less," he exhorted. But most Hondurans were already close to absolute poverty. Higher taxes, devaluation, and government budget cuts were of little help. Next to Belize, Honduras was the least industrialized Central American nation, and its small industrial sector was operating at only 50 percent capacity.

Three relics of the Contra years still fester on Honduran soil. Plentiful firearms from the garrison days of the 1980s introduced an edge of violence into a peaceful society. A black market of loot cut from supplies to the Contras has left a more aggressive black market in other things as well. Finally, although a direct link between drugs and aid to the Contras was never conclusively proved during the Oliver North hearings, Honduras became a transshipment point for the Medellín Cartel's cocaine trade. In other words, an idyllic land had begun to share some of the infirmities of the rest of the world.

The next election, at the end of 1985, although peaceful, was a game of Chinese boxes. In a political deadlock, the military intervened; this time not for a party or a favorite individual, but for the good of the country. They convened direct negotiations between presidential and congressional arbiters. The curious compromise that was reached resulted in the untroubled but constitutionally irregular election of José Azcona Hoyo.

Azcona was critical of U.S. Contra policy and tried to distance himself from the CIA's covert activities. He soon found most of his efforts absorbed by the process of seeking a Central American settlement and peace. The Contradora negotiations bogged down, and Washington resumed sending aid money to the Contras. Honduras, working earnestly for the reassimilation of the Contras into Nicaraguan society, sought a new meeting with its neighbors. By consensus the five Central American presidents met without outside advice to arrive at a strictly Central American peace, superseding the Contradora efforts. The Arias Plan, inspired by the president of Costa Rica, Oscar Arias Sánchez, emerged.

After several meetings in which Nicaragua finally joined, an agreement was signed in August 1987 that called for cessation of outside aid to insurgent forces, decrees of amnesty, negotiated cease-fires, and denial of national territories to insurgent groups. Despite the Bush administration's disapproval, after several reschedulings of the deadline, the plan was implemented and the U.S. Congress agreed to cut off the Contras' humanitarian aid if they failed to disband.

Persistent summit meetings were rewarded by a plan in 1989 that called for the demobilization and repatriation of the Contras in return for open elections in Nicaragua. In February of the next year, the internationally monitored elections resulted in the defeat of Daniel Ortega and the election of Violeta Chamorro, widow of a revered martyred newspaper publisher. The Sandanistas discovered that many of their countrymen had deeply resented their authoritarian rule.

A New Era

It was a new Honduran president who enjoyed the fruits of this resolution and the dissolution of the Contra problem. With no unconstitutional improvisations in the election process, Rafael Leonardo Callejas of the Conservative Party won a convincing victory and was free to concentrate on domestic issues. National belt-tightening was creating citizen discontent. Still saddled with IMF austerity demands and the counter pull of inflation, he faced a host of pressing needs for schools, roads, port facilities, and increased export income.

Nevertheless, the possibilities of change and forward movement were in the air. One clear plus was the completion of the El Cajón hydroelectric project—even though its income was used to pay interest on international debts. The Honduran congress, scenting a new interest in the country among outsiders, passed a host of decrees to lure tourists and encourage foreigners to reside and invest in Honduras.

Other areas were brightening, too. Textile export companies multiplied, supplying many Hondurans with low, but at least some, wages. Coffee was becoming a significant export, and shrimp farming was growing on Guanaja and the Gulf of Fonseca. Even the banana companies were improving their international image. United became Chiquita Brands, and Standard became Dole.

In 1993 a new Central American Free Trade Zone went into effect, members agreeing to reduce tariffs among themselves and create a free-trade area and customs union in the near future. On another front, the International Court of Justice finally settled the boundary dispute between Honduras and El Salvador.

Carlos Roberto Reina of the Liberal Party, the fourth democratically elected president in succession, donned the sash of office in January 1994. A 67-year-old lawyer, he had appeared before the International Court of Justice in the border dispute, had worked for international human rights organizations, and had seen the inside of the jailhouse for opposing policies of the military.

He called for a "moral revolution" to combat widespread corruption and, to the surprise of many, established a new Ministry of the Public, charged with investigating accusations of corruption and the misdeeds of military officers over the last decade. Later,

Shrimping is among many growing Honduran industries.

however, he mysteriously dissolved the commission. He promised to reduce the size of the armed forces and ended the draft, making the army volunteer. (Actually, the draft had never been the major method of induction. Impressment had been the favorite game. Now no longer would press-gangs roam the streets, "recruiting" shoeless boys into service.)

Reina inherited a large foreign debt as well as a public-sector debt equal to 10 percent of the GDP. Although he cut the budget 10 percent, he increased expenditures for social programs. A major setback was the energy crisis of 1994. A nationwide drought had lowered the water level in the Francisco Morazán Dam, the country's principal source of electricity, crippling industry with rotating blackouts. Honduras was forced to import power, leading to the eruption of public debt early in Reina's term. Punishing rises in fuel and food prices followed.

Reina supported environmental protection and vigorously encouraged ecotourism as a way to help foreign investment. In 1996 31.6 percent of the national budget was dedicated to servicing the public debt, 35 percent to social spending, and 9.2 percent to infrastructure. His moves against official corruption and assertion of civilian control over the once-powerful military incurred considerable hostility. His administration revised the Central Bank Law, better equipping the bank to modernize the national economy.

Despite greater political stability and attempts to increase social programs, the Honduran economy continues to suffer the aftereffects of the energy crisis. Less than half the population can afford to finish elementary school, and medical care for the rural population is deficient. In 1997, an estimated 67 percent of the population lived below the poverty line. Education, however, has improved. Thanks partly to American social development aid, almost 70 percent of Honduran children complete sixth grade, compared to 44 percent in 1980. But American aid has diminished sharply since the Contra years. The United States now lags behind the World Bank and Japan in support for Honduras, appropriating only $28 million last year and requesting only $23 million from Congress in 1998.

For the first time, in the November 1997 race for the presidency,

▼▲▼

a woman, Nora Gúnera de Melgar, ex-mayor of Tegucigalpa and head of the National Party, entered the list against the Liberal Party's Carlos Flores Facusse. She promised an "education revolution," wide social and economic reforms, and increased privatization of governmental activities. Nevertheless, in January 1998, Flores donned the sash of office—the first elected Liberal president since the return of democracy in 1981. He received more than 55 percent of nearly 1.9 million votes—a showing that proportionately puts our election turnouts to shame.

---

1. Federal Research Division, *Honduras: A Country Study*, third edition, ed. Tim L. Merill (Library of Congress, 1995), 13–14.

2. Clifford Krauss, *Inside Central America*, (New York: Summit Books, 1991) 181.

3. Tom Barry and Deb Preusch, *The Central American Fact Book* (New York: Grove Press, 1986), 253.

4

▼▲▼

The People

Retirees contemplating moving home and hearth to another country and spending their retirement years there will do well to consider the character and temperament of the people among whom they will live. And anyone thinking of putting down roots in that country as an investor must take into account the work habits of the people with whom he or she will be working.

Of Honduras's many attractions one of the most appealing is the people. In 1997 there are about six million Hondurans. While there is no recent census, most of them live in the western highlands and Caribbean lowlands. Generalizations about people are risky and often suspect, but a fair consensus exists of the traits and quirks of the majority of Hondurans.

Lagging far behind its neighbors in development, Honduras is still struggling to build a modern state and a unified economy, and so is still groping toward a clear image of its national identity. The picture it has presented to the outside world is that of the prototype "banana republic." No less a pen than O. Henry's sketched it as that, as a kind of primitive comic operetta country in his 1904 bestseller *Cabbages and Kings*. (Characteristically, Hondurans forgave his jibes and erected a monument to him in Trujillo where he lived for eight years.)

Indeed, historically, the Honduran has had much to forgive or at least to bear, and most often has done so with remarkable patience. Long dominated by outsiders—Spain, pirates and gunboat adventurers, banana conglomerates and powerful transnational companies, the English in the Bay Islands, the United States in the mainland, and intermittently by its own army—Honduras is a long-standing republic that has enjoyed little sovereignty or political stability.

As a consequence Hondurans have less of that fierce nationalistic pride, indeed jingoism, that has often proved troublesome for its neighbors. To die for one's country is not a national ideal. To be in dire need of foreign help is a common circumstance. Thus to the American visitor the Honduran will often seem self-deprecating and unusually accommodating.

The American Influence

Despite frequent manipulation and even intrusion by the United States, Hondurans hold the United States and Americans in high regard. Their admiration can be unexpected and often excessive. One Honduran woman, although abandoned by the American soldier who fathered her child, declared, "Americans are just nice. You see that medical clinic over there? American doctors deworm dozens of Honduran children there every day. The Americans help us. We are poor and we need them."

"Excessive" describes one Honduran matriarch's admiration of all things American. If a product comes from America, it must be perfection; if Honduran in origin, then shoddy and unreliable. Told by a friend that he had just gotten a pacemaker installed, she immediately asked, "It's American, isn't it?" When the coronary victim admitted that it was Honduran, she mourned, "Too bad! It will surely fail."

American development aid has accomplished some positive

things: Innoculations and projects to increase potable water in rural areas have reduced infant mortality. Education and road building have improved. Stone fences and terrace farming have slowed the erosion of arable land.

The trust most Hondurans have in Americans is touching but, in some cases, ill-advised. Dunia Tomé, a private school language teacher in Copán, told of an American who opened a restaurant in the area. He borrowed the equivalent of $20,000 from overly trusting Honduran acquaintances, then went on a buying spree for stereos and various expensive refinements. Within a month he suddenly abandoned the restaurant and departed the country without so much as a farewell note.

Evidence of the influence of the United States is omnipresent. Our trademarks and slogans abound. The promise and sweet tang of Coca-Cola is advertised in every *tienda*. More remarkably, if you glance out a window of the Honduras Maya Hotel at night, you will see a tall peak looming over hilly Tegucigalpa. There, reminiscent of

James D. Gollin

The American influence is everywhere.

the famed Hollywood sign, high up on the hillside, a proud Coca-Cola blazes like a beacon over the capital.

Or perhaps you pick up a snack—a popular munch called Sabritas. It takes no great linguistic ability to deduce that the inscription on the bag, "*A que no puedes comer solo una,*" is a Spanish version of "Bet you can't eat just one." Honduran poet Nelsón Merren laments that children's folktales have been replaced by Donald Duck and Superman, the marimba has given way to disco, and the traditional bakeshops have been superseded by Dunkin Donuts.

Hondurans can acquire some bad habits from foreigners, but apparently they can also unlearn them. All along the highways one sees signs in Spanish with the injunction: "Don't mistreat the signs." So what does the American driver expect to see? Graffiti, of course. And a few years ago those excrescences were all too visible. Our national plague of disfiguring all open surfaces had crept insidiously into Honduras.

But today that plague is in remission, the signs are unmarked, and the sides of buildings—except for an occasional deliberate and well-drawn mural—are pristine. A national anti-graffiti campaign apparently has worked. And Honduras's newly acquired concern for ecology has sharply diminished old ways of slash-and-burn farming and wholesale leveling of forests.

Standard of Living

Honduras is a poor country. Indeed, until the late 1980s it was poorer than all seven of its neighbors. Then the economy of Nicaragua, troubled by Sandanista fumblings and U.S. sanctions, did a nose-dive to the bottom rung. By any measure, however, Honduras is still poor. Forty percent of the population share a little under 9 percent of the wealth.

Still, what little wealth there is is distributed more evenly here than in any other Central American country. Although the old saw about the rich getting richer and the poor poorer is heard here as it is everywhere, there is less of a chasm between the haves and the have-nots and little malevolent envy. Because, until this century, the area was isolated and lacked any significant mineral deposits or other easily exploitable wealth, the colonial elite in Honduras came to be defined by their prominence in the political system rather than by their wealth. The well-to-do are not a cohesive group, frequently split on economic and social issues. The rich are not the exploiters they have been in nearby countries. And the small but growing middle class is defined as much by completion of higher education as by economic standing.

Virtually everyone in every class encounters similar difficulties in shortages of goods, interruptions of electric and water supplies, inflation, and political confusion, but Hondurans regard these annoyances with an easygoing tolerance. And poverty is so widespread as to seem unexceptional. Life for the average Honduran is hard, but he bears that hardship with remarkable patience and surprisingly good humor.

Although as much as 40 percent of the labor pool may be unemployed at times, there is no begging. Selling is the alternative of choice. Whole families unite, children tirelessly hawking shoe shines and newspapers, adults contributing imaginative variations. At bus stops along the highway, people selling fruits, vegetables, sweets, and tacos hold up their offerings in baskets on long poles. Passengers can reach them through open windows. Payment is placed in the basket, and transactions are completed with mutual trust.

One colorful type of make-work borders on begging but keeps the dignified guise of labor. After the rainy season, potholes riddle the highways and multiply exponentially in the softer surfaced byways. Honduran drivers whirl and curve around them with the grace of matadors. When the size of a hole is impressive and its location strategic, entrepreneurship take an interesting form, described appreciatively by Bill Martin, Trujillo expatriate. Two or three Indians or Caribs, armed with shovels and pails, will appear, studying the depression carefully. They will signal an oncoming car to stop, gesturing eloquently as to the size of the hazard. While the driver waits, they pack the hole with mud or clay from their buckets, flatten the mounds with the backs of their shovels, and even stamp across their repair to demonstrate its firmness. Finally, they gesture to the driver to proceed in safety—their waving hands palms upward to receive the grateful driver's tip.

Race and Gender Issues

Racism is virtually nonexistent in Honduras. Nine out of every ten Hondurans are mestizo, a mixture of Spanish and Amerindian stocks. Skin shades vary through a wide spectrum, but people of all colors mingle easily, often affectionately. Perhaps because the country was sparsely populated for centuries, its mestizo culture is quite homogeneous. Class relations don't exhibit the tensions that are so strong in neighboring countries. The shared descent of the overwhelming majority has spared Honduras the violently cruel racial divisions that have racked Guatemala, Nicaragua, and El Salvador. The accepted term for referring to the native-born population as a group is "nationals."

Machismo is bred into all Latin American males, and Honduran men share in this cult of masculinity. But that time-dishonored attitude is breaking down. Honduran men used to be scandalized by the sight of women driving cars or pickups. It was not "feminine." Today female commercial drivers are common.

Still, Honduran femininity is pronounced. Skirts are preferred over pantsuits. Among the more elite, a woman's smoking or drinking in public is considered less than top drawer, and divorce is a stigma among the very religious.

Male tyranny is not well regarded in Honduras. It is unlawful for a husband to strike his wife. Although the husband is by custom the head of the family, on many occasions the wife, "soul of the house," will take center stage and hold forth on various topics while her husband smiles approval of her eloquence.

Personalismo

Also in the mestizo culture, male arrogance is tempered by the Amerindian heritage and by *personalismo*, a genuine regard for family and for the individual. In Honduras pride and honor generally manifest themselves as a can-do attitude and a willingness to solve the problems of those needing help. An anecdote may illustrate this spirit.

Driving to Trujillo from La Ceiba, I became so engrossed in avoiding the more serious potholes and failures of the roadway—it is nonetheless true that Honduras has the best highways in Central America—I somehow missed the turnoff to town and continued merrily westward. When it finally dawned on me that I had gone too far, I called out "Trujillo?" to an Indian standing at the roadside. When he pointed firmly in the direction from which I had come, I did a U-turn. In a few moments I spotted a Texaco sign and pulled into the station for more exact information.

The three men chatting by the gas pumps agreed with friendly chuckles on the exact number of kilometers by which I had overshot the mark. On impulse I pulled out the regional map and asked if they would show me exactly where I was. (I was vaguely curious to find out if there were any interesting pueblos nearby.)

They spread the map on the hood of my car and studied it with profound seriousness. Suddenly I was embarrassed. Seeing pointing fingers zigzagging aimlessly over the entire map, I realized that they couldn't even find Trujillo, the only large city for many miles. They couldn't read and had probably never used a road map.

We were faced with two obstacles: Their machismo would not let them admit to illiteracy and their innate courtesy to strangers made them unwilling to seem unobliging. Anxious to help them save face, I stabbed at a spot somewhat to the left of the city, hoping for their easy agreement. Just then a nearby teenager, who must have

James D. Gollin

Honduran sister and brother

finished the required but hardly enforced six grades of schooling, placed a fingernail on a spot near my finger and asserted the locus. At that all three men nodded in smiling agreement and we parted with an exchange of courtesies.

According to the United Nations *Human Development Report* of 1995, three out of ten Hondurans are illiterate, and that ratio is probably higher among males. Desperate poverty causes many children to go to work with little or no schooling. Honduran law allows minors to work with the consent of both parents.

Third-world simplicity is in no way to be equated with graceless barbarism, however. In all personal dealings the feelings and dignity of the individual are considered. If you'll forgive a somewhat indelicate story, a trifling incident in Siguatepeque offers a good example.

Afflicted with a noontime thirst and the first edge of hunger, I stepped into a workingman's *comedor* (café) to enjoy a taco with trimmings and a cold bottle of domestic beer. After I had paid my small tab, I suddenly felt an urgent pressure on the bladder.

When I asked the smiling Ladino proprietor if there was a toilet on the premises, she nodded pleasantly and asked only one question: "*Solamente pee-pee?*" I reassured her in the affirmative and she escorted me to a shadowed corner of the establishment and pointed out a narrow wooden closet. Not surprisingly, there was no light inside so I was faced with the choice of exposure to the general view or inaccuracy in the total darkness. She backed away discreetly as I compromised by leaving the door cracked open.

When I was finished I pressed the flush lever in vain. When I complained that the mechanism did not function, she seemed undismayed and gestured that I should wait. She picked up a ladle and a small basin from a four-foot urn of water, and held the basin under my hands while ladling water over them with the ceremony of an altar boy washing a priest's hands during Mass. As I dried with the towel she gave me, she took a larger ladle full of water into the closet and took care of sanitation. We parted smiling in mutual good will.

The thoughtfulness and courtesy that Hondurans show to

strangers seem to fail in only two circumstances: on the highway and, as Trujillo resident Bill Martin points out, in a lineup for a queue. Hondurans apparently feel gifted with eyes that see around corners, for they will speed past you on mountain curves unblemished by guardrails. And when a sudden change requires a second approach to a counter—as in the not infrequent cancellation of a flight—the rush to repurchase or renegotiate is headlong. There is no bowing deference to prior claims. The pushing is determined, and the inexperienced traveler finds himself contemplating dozens of squirming backs that have somehow wriggled past him.

A Peaceful Land

Blessedly free of the bloody wars and internecine savagery that have afflicted its neighbors, except for its four-day Soccer War with El Salvador, Honduras has no tradition of violence. Even during those intervals when the army assumed control of the country, the coups were almost always bloodless and the rule usually tolerant rather than harsh.

For generations Honduras has been praised for its peacefulness and nonviolence and for the safety it has promised the foreign traveler. Today, unfortunately, that boast lacks its former total assurance. Since the United States used Honduras as a platform for its support of the Contras, there have been discernible changes. Some of the drug traffic has shifted from Panama. Armed robberies and muggings, although comparatively rare, are no longer unheard of. While most foreign residents are not worried, some will warn you about certain sectors after nightfall.

A few incidents of youth gangs, although not very well organized, have been reported. The theft of valuable religious treasures scandalized many in 1996. Bars have appeared on residences of the well-to-do, armed "watchies" patrol their grounds at night, and shutters come down over the windows of upscale shops.

The visitor can no longer be totally carefree. Longtime expatriate residents are grieved to see the electronic doorway and armed guards in the American Embassy in Tegucigalpa. Honduras has come, however slightly, to resemble the rest of the modern world. But, again comparatively, the country is still a haven from the much greater ills of the rest of the hemisphere, and visitors feel safe.

Even in times of stress and armed menace, native Honduran warmth and peaceful instincts somehow emerge. In September 1982 Honduran malcontents first tried terrorist tactics. A small band of "liberation" guerrillas burst into a meeting of the Chamber of Commerce in San Pedro Sula, firing assault rifles and ordering all business leaders and government officials to hit the floor. The amateur terrorists released all sick and wounded hostages immediately, but the siege lasted eight days. During it, a crowd of more than 20,000 people demonstrated outside *against* the guerrillas, chanting *"Honduras sí, Terrorismo no!"* Between popular disapproval and the impasse resulting from cutting off water and telephones, the captors dropped all demands in exchange for a plane ride to Cuba. The chief distinction between this hostage situation and those in all other countries was noted by a reporter on the scene: "The hostages and their keepers coexisted well. The hostages elected representatives, and after a while they played cards and told jokes with the rebels.

THE MAYAN PROPHECY

Throughout all this talk of retirement and future possibilities, the ancient Mayans cast a somber cloud. Mayan mythology held that the cosmos appears and disappears again and again, in an odd parallel to the expanding, shrinking, and reemerging universes of the "Big Bang" theory.

One Mayan calendar traces the creation of the present world—its fourth creation, marked by beings who would do the gods adequate honor—to our year 3114 B.C. That same calendar dates this world as ending in the very close year of A.D. 2012! In our talk about retirement, are we assuming too long a future?

These weren't the kind of guerrillas you find in El Salvador or Guatemala. They didn't insult, offend, or abuse anyone physically. Hondurans are a kind, open people."[1]

Last but by no means least, most North Americans are startled by their first exposure to the mañana philosophy prevalent in all of Latin America. Hondurans have a very fluid sense of time, and tomorrow often offers the preferred occasion for action. Once one becomes used to this unfamiliar leisure, it is very relaxing. And if the Hondurans are somewhat casual about the clock, they are all the more generous with their time. If you need time with a Honduran, he or she has time for you.

A Brief Demography

The mestizos, or Ladinos, form the largest racial group, numbering an estimated 90 percent of the population. Amerindians are the next largest group. These *indígenas* are descendants of those who ruled the land five centuries ago until the Spanish colonists pushed them aside, subjected them to forced labor, and communicated a variety of European diseases that decimated them. Most of those who survived intermarried with their conquerors, but several hundred thousand have managed to retain their original languages, culture, and social structures. The present Honduran government, to its credit, is encouraging the preservation of these people, their languages, and their ways.

Most numerous of those identifiably Indian are the Lencas, related to the Mayas, scattered through the highlands of the southwest. Their common language has almost disappeared, but many continue to make their distinctive baskets, ceramics, and home brew, while others till communal lands and still others serve as itinerant coffee pickers. A considerable number can be found in and around the charming town of La Esperanza to the southwest of Comayagua. These were the people who, with their chief Lempira, first offered a determined resistance to the conquistadors.

The Misquitos (or Miskitos) live in small isolated communities in the north, the Mosquito Coast, shared with Nicaragua. Descendants of South American Indians, they hunt, fish, grow root crops, and speak in their native tongue. For centuries they were allies of the English, some of whose black slaves intermarried with their ancestors. Other peoples in this area are the Pech, or Paya, in the western part, known for their close relationship with nature.

In the northeast are the endangered Tolupanes, now forgetful of their 5,000-year-old pre-Mayan language, barely subsisting on a hunter-gatherer economy. The government has created what it calls the Tawahka Biosphere Reserve to preserve large tracts of virgin forest and its threatened inhabitants, the Tawahka Indians, now marginal survivors because of deforestation and encroachment. To the west around Copán live the Chortis, descendants of the Maya who have lost their ancestral tongue.

Blacks make up perhaps 2 percent of Honduras's total population. Most distinctive are the 100,000 Garifunas, or Black Caribs, living in small communities on the islands and along the Caribbean coast. Oddly enough, a far greater number of them now inhabit New York. One story of their origin tells that survivors of a shipwreck of African slaves intermarried with "Red Carib" natives on the island of St. Vincent and that their descendants were later deported to the Bay Islands, long under British dominion. Their numbers were increased by slaves escaping from the buccaneers of Port Royal.

The Bay Island Garifunas have retained their distinct identity. They all speak some English—in addition to their own language, a Carib-based Creole—and most speak Spanish as a third language. (Instruction in the Garifuna language and folklore is available in Trujillo through Belinda Linton's language school.) Shrimpers, carvers, boat builders, and sometime smugglers, they also raise roots such as yams and manioc. In their seaside thatched huts, often elevated on pilings above shallow water, they have retained many African elements in their folklore, music, and religion. Although nominally Catholic, their religious

▼▲▼▲▼▲▼▲▼▲▼▲▼▲▼▲▼▲▼

**HONDURAN
POPULATION STATISTICS**

mestizos:	90 percent
Ameridians:	7 percent
blacks:	2 percent
whites:	1 percent

▲▼▲▼▲▼▲▼▲▼▲▼▲▼▲▼▲▼▲

practices show African influences and a hint of voodoo. On Christmas and New Year's their all-night, masked "Johnny Canoe" dance is spectacular. For musical instruments, they use a kind of pipe gong, maracas, and drums made of turtle and conch skeletons. Marion Seaman, American publisher of Roatán's *Coconut Telegraph,* notes that their dances are for their dead—important forces in guiding the living. On Punta Gorda on Roatán, they give shows every Saturday. The rhythm of their dance-song, the *punta,* is widely popular and imitated by dance bands on the mainland.

White people, about 1 percent of the total, have lived in Honduras since the Spanish conquest. Those on the mainland have either merged into the Ladino culture or at least mingle freely within it. Those native to the islands speak English and consider themselves British rather than Honduran. They sport their distinctly English surnames proudly, like badges of honor, as do many of the black islanders.

A third group of whites, often called Arabs, or Turcos because they first entered on Turkish passports, are businessmen from Lebanon and neighboring countries who have found opportunities for profitable investment in Honduras. This group alone may encounter some bias because a number of Hondurans regard them as money-hungry hustlers. Most of Honduras was shocked recently by whispered slurs directed against Carlos Flores Facusse–called a Turco because of Palestinian forebears on his mother's side.

A small but growing number of Tawainese and Koreans, most of whom work in garment assembly plants, complete the tally of recognizable ethnic groups. Honduras has variety but the mix blends well.

---

1. Clifford Krauss, *Inside Central America,* (New York, Summit Books, 1991), 191.

5

▼▲▼▲▼▲▼▲▼▲▼▲▼▲▼▲▼▲▼▲▼▲▼▲▼▲▼▲▼▲▼▲▼▲▼▲▼▲▼

Money Matters

Your principal concern is probably whether you have enough money for retirement. If it isn't, and your chief worry is "Who will I be when I'm no longer the manager of the McDonald's of East Wichita?" then my advice is not to retire. Your individuality is still defined by your job. With patience and time you will find your real self.

Assuming that your retirement fund is your concern and a more idyllic life is your dream, I imagine that you have already sent that postcard supplied by your insurance company to Box 57 in Baltimore, requesting a statement of earnings and an estimate of entitlement benefits. You've checked pension rights, Keogh plans, IRAs, 401(k), bank accounts, CDs, annuities, and your stock and bond holdings.

You've added the numbers up and perhaps are disappointed. The total return may be far below the 80 percent of present income that financial advisors and glib money magazines say is adequate for retiring. (They benignly allow a 20 percent knockoff on the theory that you'll spend less for transportation, office attire, office "charity" contributions, and mandatory rubber chicken dinners.)

The fact of the matter is, whether you're a McDonald's manager at $40,000 or a CEO at $90,000, you probably haven't been able to reach that 80 percent in sure post-retirement income. So what do you do? Grind away and die in the saddle? Retire but remain where you are, as most retirees do, with a greatly compromised lifestyle? Or do you find some place to retire pleasurably for only a fraction of that ideal income?

If your last birthday cake had 60 candles on it, you should know that every insurance company is willing to bet that you have at least another 20 years ahead. You have another third of your life to live. Don't let the "senior citizen" tag depress you. Instead let it focus your thoughts on how best to spend what Hondurans gracefully call the "third age."

When to Retire

Want to retire a bit early? How about at age 62? Are you worried about what that will do to your pension and Social Security payment? I can't answer for your pension but, as to the 3 percent reduction in Social Security payments for each year before age 65, don't worry. It will be 18 years before the righteous 65-year-old retiree catches up with you in *total* cash disbursements, because you've been drawing for three years when he wasn't! On the other side of the coin, however, is the fact that Medicare doesn't kick in until you attain the full flower of 65 years. Moreover, your COLA (inflation) increases, because in percents, will be less.

You may wish to retire a bit later. Social Security adds about 3 percent to your monthly check for each year that you defer retirement after age 65. Presently the administration estimates that its retirement checks come to about 42 percent of the preretirement earnings of the average wage earner and 26 percent of the former salary of a high wage earner.

The absolute minimum check in all states is $484 per month,

to most Hondurans the income of the well-to-do, but a small fraction of the amount needed by most Americans to even consider retiring near their old stamping grounds. Nonworking spouses receive half the monthly benefit of the working partner. Working spouses can choose the half-benefit or the income they have earned by working. You need not worry about receiving those moneys abroad. Social Security follows you wherever you go except to Cuba, Cambodia, North Korea, Vietnam, and some of the former Soviet republics. For other specifics about your Social Security options, a daytime call to Social Security (800-772-1213) will reach a service representative.

Don't Forget Inflation

One vital consideration regarding those retirement dollars is their worth, not just their number. Inflation is the termite that nibbles away at even proverbial wooden nickels, and its bite grows by the voracity of compounding. At a projected 3 percent annual inflation rate, your present dollar would shrink to a half-dollar in 24 years. Even if we project an optimistic inflation rate of only 2 percent annually, the item you buy for a dollar when you retire will cost a dollar and a half in 20 years. And if you retire early enough to hope for an additional 30 years at the same low inflation rate, every thousand dollars you have at retirement will be worth only $545 then.

There are, however, reassuring considerations. The value of your Social Security checks remain approximately constant so long as Congress continues the COLA (inflation) increases. Your pension check shouldn't suffer either, for any decent pension fund should earn enough to compensate over the years.

The danger lies in your savings. It is the disposition of any nest egg you have tucked away that deserves scrutiny. If you hope to hatch it in a fixed return instrument such as bonds, that return will shrink in value year by year.

But, you rightly object, won't I face the erosion of inflation wherever in the world I go? Surely Honduras has suffered from inflation? Indeed it has. But your move to Honduras offers a hidden compensation. That secret is the rate of exchange.

Exchange Rates

The coin of the realm in Honduras is the lempira (L), named after that heroic Amerindian chieftain of 1537. Almost all goods and services are paid for in lempiras. Exceptions are a few dive centers and posh resort hotels in the Bay Islands, Tegucigalpa, and San Pedro Sula, where credit cards or travelers checks in American dollars are strongly preferred. In discussing costs, I nonetheless quote prices in American dollars—both because American money is probably familiar to you and because the dollar is much more stable than the devalued and shrinking lempira.

As I write this paragraph in April 1998 the official rate of exchange is 13.17L for $1. So each lempira is worth about 7.5 cents. In December 1993, in an attempt at stabilization, the official exchange was set at 7.26L. Shortly afterward, deregulated, the lempira was freed to float to more realistic levels. In the next two and a half years the rate jumped 50 percent. In the last two years the gain has totaled less than 19 percent. Clearly Honduran inflation is moderating. In February 1997 and March 1998, the lempira actually gained slightly against the buck.

The dollar-holder occupies the catbird seat. Honduran inflation has generally been balanced by the devaluation of the lempira. To make that advantage clearer, consider a comparison using the economist's favorite product, the widget. So long as I make my exchanges into lempiras gradually, the widget that I could buy for $1 in December 1993 I can still buy for little more than $1 today, although the price tag may have been altered from 7.25L to a tad over 13L.

The trick lies in gradual, only-as-needed exchanges. Of course, if I deposit enough dollars in a Honduran bank to cover a whole year's living expenses, exchanging it all at once for lempiras, I will feel the Honduran economy's inflation throughout that year.

The current official exchange rate is published daily in newspapers. Airport exchanges are usually the visitor's first stop to obtain local currency, but a modest amount should suffice, for airports and banks usually give a slightly less advantageous rate than do the exchange houses (*casas de cambio*) advertised in *Honduras This Week.* Hotels also change money, but usually at a less than generous rate.

The best rate is often offered on the black market, officially tolerated despite the ominous name. Usually dealers pay 1 or 2 percent above the day's official exchange, but sometimes they offer rates below par, especially on weekends or after banking hours. As of April 1998 they were offering 13.22L, $1/20$ of a lempira more than the offical rate—probably not worth the risk. Dealers with fans of banknotes and handheld calculators appear in every airport and at central locations in the cities. If you deal with them, be cautious—at least until you have become familiar with the currency and have acquired Honduran street smarts.

Banking

Traveler's checks are best converted in banks and *casas de cambio.* Your passport and sometimes your driver's license may be needed for identification. Some banks are fussy: I've heard that Banco de Honduras likes only Citicorp traveler's checks and that Creditlan's service charge is high. Prudent travelers make sufficient exchanges on weekdays to last over the weekend, although many banks are open on Saturday morning.

A credit card is useful. Visa, Master Card, and American Express are generally accepted and can be used for car rentals and upscale restaurants and hotels, thus cutting down the amount of cash you need to carry. In a pinch most banks will give a cash advance on a credit card (*retiro de tarjeta de crédito*). Look for a "Credomatic" sign in a bank, or for the office with that name in Tegucigalpa.

Once you establish a Honduran bank account, you can arrange to wire transfer your Social Security and/or pension checks. You will also receive Honduran bank credit cards, which you can use at the relatively few ATMs in Honduras. Honduran ATMs are not usually compatible with American systems. Not surprisingly, a personal check drawn on an American bank is difficult to cash.

Be prepared for Third-World ways and green-eyeshade technology in some of the banks. Karen Schrey, who along with her husband represents J. Edwards Real Estate on Roatán, told me of her first encounter with an island bank. Shortly after the Schreys arrived and managed to find a rental house, they opened an account at a local bank and proceeded to lose themselves in a flurry of check writing. Things can get confusing when you're dealing with two currencies at once. So it was a welcome call they received from the bank manager, assuring them that their account had been balanced and that they could check on it with a visit to the bank. They knew by this time not to expect the computerized statement they were accustomed to in the States. But when Karen arrived at the bank, the manager presented her with two shoeboxes full of handwritten accounts. Her assignment, with the help of a smiling bank teller, was to finger her way through the boxes until she came to her account. Talk about keeping up with the Joneses! She had ample opportunity, if she cared to pry, to note what the Joneses earned and what they paid for just about everything they bought. The statement of her account, when she found it after a painstaking search, proved accurate and meticulous in every handwritten detail.

Seasoned travelers in Honduras try to always have some American banknotes on hand. As a gift to an intransigent official, the dollar of appropriate denomination is magic. And, if you temporarily run short of the local currency, most hotels, large restaurants, and even taxi drivers accept U.S. banknotes. A few tens, fives, and ones can come in handy.

Money transfers within the country can be difficult. Computers are still relatively new. Most expatriates in Honduras leave the bulk of their money in banks in the United States or the Cayman Islands, as bank checks from these sources are recognized and approved.

Canadians and Europeans usually convert their money into U.S. dollars at home. Lloyds Banks in Tegucigalpa and San Pedro Sula will exchange pounds, marks, and Canadian dollars, but at a pretty price. In other parts of the country European bills are regarded with suspicion, as if they could be forgeries. Conversion of other foreign moneys is a near impossibility.

▾▲▾

Honduran banknotes are color coded, ranging from the orange 100, blue 50, green 20, black 10, and brown 5 to the humble red single. The hundred (roughly $7.60 at present) is the largest banknote. Because of the devaluation of the currency, there are few coins. Most common are the 50 centavo and the 20 centavo, called a *daime* because it is the size of the American dime. It's worth about 1½ cents.

Cost of Living

"Okay, so the currency is colorful," you say, "but what kind of living will these Technicolor banknotes buy me?" That's a good question, and the answer depends on a number of variables. If you insist on living in one of the tourist hot spots like the center of the Bay Island of Roatán, you'll need at least 20 percent more than you would on the mainland. Besides the way tourism puffs up prices, there's the simple necessity of importing every commodity sold on the islands from the mainland.

International Living promises that a single person can retire comfortably in Honduras on $600 a month and that a couple can be comfortable with $1,000 a month. That's a bit optimistic if those figures include the cost of housing on the Bay Islands and big cities, because lately rents have increased significantly in Roatán, San Pedro Sula, and the capital, Tegucigalpa.

But assuming you've snared a bargain rental contract or have already built living quarters, then those figures are high. Numbers like those will enable you to go out to eat and drink most evenings, have a live-in housekeeper if you have enough room, buy food, clothing, and ordinary necessities, recreate moderately, and travel a little.

Honduras on the Cheap

Let's start at the low end of the financial scale with the retiree who is looking at an income of about $600 a month from his Social Security for the rest of his life, with small annual increases to compensate for U.S. inflation. Not a happy prospect for survival in New York or San Francisco—not much happier in Ohio or Montana either.

But you can make do on that $600 with fair ease in the smaller towns on mainland Honduras. You can rent a small apartment or hotel room with private bath and maid service for $150 to $200 per month and manage on the remainder. If your company has a pension plan that pays you, say, $400 more per month, the total of $1,000 would allow you to do very well, even in the mainland cities.

You won't pay any Honduran income tax on money received from the United States. If you do get a job in Honduras you'll pay income tax on any annual salary over 20,000L, or about $125 a month.

Buying a Home

If you've succeeded in squirreling away a nest egg of $25,000 or $30,000 or can clear that much on the sale of your U.S. home or condo, you'll be able to buy or build a two-bedroom mainland house on a quarter-acre plot alive with flowers and tropical greenery. You will have to come up with spot cash, for Honduran banks see the mortgage business as too uncertain and speculative with the continual fluctuation of the lempira. Exceptionally, you might arrange financing with the owner, paying close to half the price in cash down with a one- or two-year term to come up with the balance at, say, 12 percent interest.

On $600 per month Social Security you probably won't be able to afford to buy, build, or reside on the popular Bay Islands of Roatán or Guanaja. The modest but pleasant 1,200-square-foot concrete-block house with wooden deck or porch that you might build in most areas of the mainland for $25,000 could cost over $70,000 on Roatán. The price difference is mainly due to higher property costs, the need to ferry the building materials, and the higher pay scale expected by Bay Island workmen. Building on Guanaja might cost 10 to 20 percent less than on Roatán and considerably less if you build from native treated pine rather than concrete blocks.

In the last three or four years land prices on Roatán have doubled and in some places tripled. According to *International Living* there are almost no beachfront bargains left anywhere in the West

End. A three-quarter-acre tract with 100 feet of gleaming sand in this prestigious area goes for $200,000. Some Realtors insist that you can still buy a modest quarter-acre lot for only $10,000, but those lots are apt to be far from the water in densely wooded sectors.

On the undeveloped East End you'll find pirate coves, deserted beaches, and shaded hilltop sites for as little as $9,000 an acre, but often they'll be accessible only by dirt road or, in some cases, by boat. The inferior infrastructure means that you'll need to clear an access road and bring in utilities. The clearing and hauling will add considerably to the cost of building, bringing the total to between $60 and $70 per square foot.

The island of Guanaja still has some acreage with bits of beachfront for about $35,000 per quarter acre, but building there can be as costly as on Roatán. You must build a road uphill from the shore to your house, you will have to run in electricity and water, and all supplies come by LST-type boats. The price of land drops sharply as you climb the wooded hillsides away from the shore.

On Utila's beautiful but remote beachfront on the other side of the lagoon, total cost can run even higher and there are the same supply and travel difficulties. In the town itself, however, inexpensive rentals or purchases can be found. An average-size lot may go for as little as $20,000. Building costs just outside of town tend to be lower than on the other two islands because the proximity to mainland La Ceiba reduces shipping expense and a slightly lower pay scale prevails.

The beautiful beaches of the hotter and less developed North Coast are far more economical. Birkie Campbell, a European retiree and developer just outside Trujillo, sells lots with roads, electricity, and fresh water (all important considerations). Ninety-thousand dollar houses there include two stories; rooms with high ceilings, rosewood beams, and fans; sunken showers in marble bathrooms; handmade tile floors and roofs; and 2,000 square feet of space kept cool year-round by double adobe walls.

Lots with some beachfront near Trujillo are still available for a few thousand dollars, but you must build an access road to the main road and bring in your electricity and water. More inexpensive still, at prices as low as $1,500 for two-thirds of an acre, is land on the hillsides fronting the sea. Once you have a site you can arrange to build a wooden house for about $16 per square foot.

For the retiree with a bit more income and nest egg, the options are varied and alluring. On the Bay Islands today you can no longer get your dream house on a garden plot for a song (unless you happen to be one of the Three Tenors), but you can find attractive finished houses for $50,000 and up. At last report there were five well-designed subdivisions with pleasant homes offering proximity to the beach at median prices of $100,000.

In most of Honduras you can buy land and build for prices not seen in the United States in nearly 50 years. And you can rent while you're overseeing the construction. Pleasant furnished cabins owned by hotels in Roatán's West End charge $500 to $800 per month. Furnished apartments near Coxen Hole or French Harbor go for less. On the North Coast cut those figures in half. And no matter how far from the sand you are, Honduran law allows beach access for all residents.

Buying a house need not confine you to Honduras all year. A fair number of Americans who have gained legal residency live in

James D. Gollin

The Roatán coast, one of the most desirable living areas in Honduras

Honduras for half to two-thirds of the year and return annually to the States to catch up with families and friends. On the islands and in the cities, the shortage of good rental properties is such that you'll find it easy and gainful to rent your Honduran haven whenever the urge to travel overtakes you.

Or you might do what Eric Anderson, owner of the French Harbor Yacht Club, does: swap houses. Eric, a skiing buff, spends winters at a friend's house in Colorado. In exchange, his friend escapes the icy blasts of home for an idyllic month on Roatán. Or you might time-share a villa in the Sundancer Cabanas, for instance, and enjoy the beach and diving life for part of the year. They're not cheap—$20,000 per quarter—but they do give you joint ownership of such property as a 300-foot pier and thatched cabana bar.

A one-story house of treated native pine can be built on the mainland for as little as $15 per square foot. Concrete block construction, usually with floors of oak, roofs of tile, and finished with stucco in earth tones, runs about 50 percent more, averaging $25 per square foot in most suburban areas. On the Bay Islands prices range from $40 to $60 per square foot, depending on location and special needs in the area.

There are important questions to be asked in any area: Is there safe freshwater? Will you be able to sink a good well on your property or build a cistern? How far will you need to run a road and what type of surfacing does the local climate demand? Since there is no such thing as title insurance in Honduras, how secure and well-researched is your title?

Eating Out

A good steak with a choice of vegetables will cost about $7 in a fine restaurant almost anywhere in Honduras, providing you're not dining in top-drawer restaurants at the resort hotels. Even there, you'll find prices much more reasonable than in the fashionable eateries of the big cities in the States. And in the cafés that do not aim at tourists but serve the local businessmen, you will find prices considerably lower. Usually that price includes a soup or salad, sometimes a

▼▲▼

dessert. A good local beer with the main course will cost about
50 cents. A glass of good Chilean wine will run about $1.50; a bottle
costs about $5. If you order steak it will probably not be the finest
local beef, for those cuts are usually exported. It will be both tasty
and juicy, but it may be a bit stringy.

There's a lot of ocean around Honduras. Shrimp boats bring in
not only delicious shrimp but an abundance of crabs, lobsters, fish,
and other seafood. A lobster dinner with all the trimmings and a
choice of spices costs about $10. If the menu says *servicio incluído*,
there's no need to tip, but if you are pleased with your waiter toss
in a few lempiras as a gesture. Otherwise, 10 percent is the usual
tip in restaurants, although many nationals do not tip at all.

And, no, one never escapes the sales tax—anywhere. It's 7 percent on meals and 10 percent on cocktails. In most places, however,
the tax is already included in the price.

If you're on a budget, you should have little trouble eating satis-
factorily on about $15 a day with a hearty breakfast for $3, a $4
lunch, and an $8 dinner with a beer. You can eat out all the time on
about $450 a month.

And you can drink very inexpensively if you stick to rum and the
four locally produced beers: Nacional, Salva Vida, Imperial, and Port
Royal. The first two are similar to Budweiser, the latter two have
more body. I have heard of, but not tasted, a new beer being introduced by a German company, Holstein. The domestic rum is Flor de
Caña, but imports from neighboring countries are widely available.
Undistinguished gins and so-so vodkas of local origin are also inexpensive. Everywhere in Honduras, except for the upscale hotels, a
bottle of beer costs 40 to 60 cents, and rum drinks run slightly more.

Smokers can find decent domestic cigarettes for 40 cents a pack.
The high quality of Honduran cigars is beginning to attract the
attention of trendy magazines for cigar aficionados.

Eating In

As in the States, if you cook at home you'll save money. A couple can
spend as little as $200 per month eating home-cooked meals topped

off with cups of very good mountain-grown Honduran coffee.

A two-pound lobster from the market costs about $2. Prices for other foods and necessities are also low: chopped beef is $1.10 per pound, pot-roast grade beef $1.25, breast of veal $1.35, pork sausage $1.50, and picnic ham $2.20. Flour, corn flour, and rice range from 40 to 60 cents per kilo (a bit over 2 pounds). Pasta and fresh-baked coconut bread run about 50 cents per pound. Most vegetables cost about 50 cents per kilo. Soap is 25 cents per bar, and four rolls of toilet paper cost 55 cents.

Of course, if you insist on American imports you'll pay $3 for a box of Kellogg's Corn Flakes or a can of Comet. If you're devoted to Rice-a-Roni in a country that lives on its own grains, your tab is $1.50 for seven ounces. A 42-ounce box of Tide costs $7. So stick with domestic products and produce.

Native markets usually charge less for fruits and vegetables than do the supermarkets. Though there's not much difference in price for meats and seafood. As a rule, your live-in Honduran housekeeper or maid (who should earn about $60 per month) will pay less than you will, especially if you look like a foreigner.

GROCERY COSTS

pork sausage:	$1.50/pound
chopped beef:	$1.10/pound
lobster:	$1.00/pound
pasta:	50 cents/pound
vegetables:	25 cents/pound
rice:	20 cents/pound

Street Vendors

Some items are offered by street vendors for bargain prices. With widespread urban unemployment and a scarcity of good jobs, this type of informal retail business enables many entrepreneurs to keep self-respect and bread on the table. When making a purchase from a sidewalk vendor, be courteous. It is generally true that there are American prices and there are Honduran prices. Such discrimination is not illegal in Honduras. Foreign residents accept this and usually find a way to reach a fair midpoint between the two price structures.

It is said that the first two Spanish words the American tourist learns south of the border are *cuanto* (How much?) and *demasiado* (Too much). But while the tourist in Honduras may be tempted to haggle as he might in Mexico or Guatemala—where the asking price is usually double the expected result—many Hondurans are offended by haggling and resist the histrionics it entails. If a reduced price is to be offered, the vendor prefers to initiate it himself. If you express interest in some merchandise but turn away after polite thanks, he may quickly suggest a second figure (10 or 20 percent lower but never half). The prospective buyer then accepts or refuses, and the ball remains in the vendor's court. Vendors do not pursue you; they are not beggars. You will rarely see a beggar in Honduras. Panhandling is against the law.

Household Goods

A washer and dryer imported from the States to the mainland will cost about 25 percent more than in America, more if imported to the islands. Another option is to take your laundry to a nearby house where the señora may wash and fold it for about $1.50. Of course, if you plan to become a legal resident and have a washer and dryer in the home you're selling in the States, it makes sense to ship them, and the rest of your household furnishings, to Honduras duty-free.

Money Isn't Everything

There are more aspects to money matters in Honduras, but they are considered in later chapters, especially "Investment and Work in Honduras." Until then, revel in thoughts of how far your dollar can stretch if you retire in Honduras.

Still, money isn't everything. More important is your quality of life and the degree to which it suits your temperament. The expatriates I've met in Honduras assure me that they'd live there even if it weren't such a bargain!

6

▼▲▼▲▼▲▼▲▼▲▼▲▼▲▼▲▼▲▼▲▼▲▼▲▼▲▼▲▼▲▼▲▼▲▼▲▼▲▼

Health and Medicine

N o vaccination or other extraordinary health measures are necessary for entry into Honduras, nor for expatriate residents. On a first trip the cautious may wish to call the United States Center for Disease Control in Atlanta, Georgia (404-639-3311), for news of any recent outbreaks or epidemics. Or write to the Superintendent of Documents in Washington for the $6 global rundown, *Health Information for International Travelers*. Your present doctor may suggest a tetanus booster or, in some cases, shots against hepatitis and typhoid. If you plan to spend time on the islands, coast, or especially in the jungles, antimalarial pills are advisable.

The one piece of bad news about medical matters in Honduras is that, unlike your dogged Social Security checks that follow you faithfully, Medicare does not extend beyond the borders of the United States and its territories, nor do the HMOs dependent on Medicare. American health insurance policies usually do make provisions for the resident abroad, but it's wise to check that feature in your policy before going even for a visit.

Despite Medicare's refusal to travel with you, I strongly urge you to apply for Medicare Part A three months before you turn 65. Apply even if you plan to continue working for a while. Part A costs you nothing, and if you become ill before you become an immigrant, it pays substantially—80 percent of what Medicare considers an appropriate fee—towards hospitalization, skilled nursing care, hospice, and other cares. Even after you have established residence in Honduras, you may need extensive hospitalization or complicated surgery and opt to return to your old turf to receive treatment. Your Part A will come in very handy then.

Part B is voluntary but most people enroll in it. It does cost—about $43 a month is nicked from your monthly retirement check. This plan covers generous portions of bills from doctors and some other practitioners, some therapy, and a host of tests and X rays. It is no help with the dentist. This feature will not relocate with you either, so you may want to weigh the merits of joining. Besides, the standard of medical care in Honduras is high and the costs are low.

Honduran Health Care

If you are under 61 and a resident of Honduras when applying, you can get Honduran health insurance. You will be covered for a lifetime amount of $2 million. Unfortunately, the policy lapses when you turn 70. There is an HMO in Tegucigalpa. Contact SANITAS in that city.

Medical resources are readily available, especially on the Honduran mainland. Honduras's public health service lists 33 hospitals and more than 1,000 doctors. You will find that health care on the mainland is of very high quality and startlingly inexpensive. A visit to the doctor costs between $5 and $15, even though many physicians received their training in the United States. If your Spanish is meager or missing, do not worry. Many Honduran doctors speak fluent English.

Dentists also are very affordable: A bridge will cost $100. A gold crown and repair of a chipped tooth cost Dick Thomas, a new resident, $60. Fillings range between $10 and $20. One expatriate reported having dental work done for $150. She'd had an estimate in the States of at least $450 for the same work.

Drugstores (*farmacias*) are numerous and reliable. Like Mexican pharmacies they are unbelievably inexpensive because they are allowed by law a profit margin just a hair over 21 percent. And, if you are a *jubilado* (a retiree who has passed his 65th birthday), you are entitled to a mandatory 25 percent discount. Prescription drugs can cost as little as one-fifth of their stateside price. Many medications that require a prescription in the States, such as antibiotics and Valium, are sold over the counter in Honduras. But don't expect learned advice on medicines from the person who waits on you. Pharmacies are manned by sales clerks, not pharmacists.

MEDICAL PRECAUTIONS

Must-have supplies:
- sunscreen
- insect repellant
- bottled water

And if your doctor recommends:
- tetanus booster
- hepatitis shot
- typhoid shot
- antimalarial pills

A private hospital room runs between $30 and $40 per day at most hospitals, and major surgery will seldom set you back more than $1,000. Consider that the Medicare you left behind makes you pay the first $100 of your medical expenses in a given year and thereafter covers only 80 percent of what it estimates is a fair and usual charge for the treatment you received, regardless of your bills. You will almost certainly conclude that in Honduras you can take care of hospital and doctor bills for the 20 percent and the $100 you would have had to pay back home anyway.

Louis Shimkin, an American jubilado in Honduras, warns that an American's first impression of the hospital in Tegucigalpa will be of its shabbiness—walls needing paint and furnishings showing signs of rust. But he says these superficial turnoffs are no indication of the

▼▲▼▲▼▲▼▲▼▲▼▲▼▲▼▲▼▲▼▲▼▲▼▲▼▲▼▲▼▲▼▲▼▲▼▲▼▲▼

quality of the medical care—which is high. He alternates residences between Florida and Honduras, but has no compunction about using Honduran care when he's there.

The Bay Islands are hardly a medical center. Guanaja and Utila have clinics presided over by physician's assistants. Roatán has recently opened a 30-room hospital, but for serious medical emergencies most expatriates on the islands fly to the mainland. The local Methodist church on Roatán maintains a 24-hour medical transport plane.

Medicine on the mainland is competent, caring, and fairly up to date. One of the very best hospitals in Central America is the D'Antoni Hospital in La Ceiba, run by Dole (formerly Standard Brands), a very progressive employer giving its workers medical and retirement benefits. Many on the hospital staff speak English. The hospital in San Pedro Sula boasts an MRI. Both San Pedro Sula and Tegucigalpa have CAT-scanners. These three large cities are your best bet for attending to any complex medical needs. All have emergency rooms, and the Red Cross arranges ambulance pickups and other emergency services. Red Cross headquarters are in Comayaguela (tel. 443-0707 or 237-8654).

A curious cautionary note comes from *International Living*. It advises getting a written agreement from your medical practitioner

▼▲▼▲▼▲▼▲▼▲▼▲▼▲▼▲▼▲▼▲▼▲▼▲▼▲▼▲▼▲▼▲▼▲▼▲▼▲▼

MAJOR MEDICAL CENTERS

Comayaguela	Red Cross headquarters, 443-0707 or 237-8654
La Ceiba	D'Antoni Hospital, 443-2264
Guanaja, Utila, Roatán	local Methodist church maintains a 24-hour medical transport plane to the mainland and D'Antoni Hospital
Tegucigalpa	Hospital Clinica Viera, 238-0736 or 238-0696
San Pedro Sula	Semesa, 556-7401

▲▼▲▼▲▼▲▼▲▼▲▼▲▼▲▼▲▼▲▼▲▼▲▼▲▼▲▼▲▼▲▼▲▼▲▼▲▼▲

before beginning. The article cites one instance of extensive dental work, verbally estimated at less than $100, being billed for $140. Although the higher price was about one-fifth of the cost of the same work in the United States, the patient still felt "taken" because of the discrepancy between estimate and final figure.

If Third-World technology makes you nervous, Jim McDonnell's accident may reassure you. Jim, a resident of one of the smaller islands off Honduras for 16 years, is a bush pilot who frequently totes freight to and from the Mosquitia. On one trip he severed a finger at the joint in an accident. The fingertip was hanging on by a thread of skin. A Honduran surgeon, working with no more advanced tool than a jeweler's loupe, reattached it, stitching it back on so skillfully that Jim has recovered all feeling and almost total flexibility.

Sun and Insects

On the Bay Islands and on the north coast you need have no fear of lizards, iguanas, parrots, or ratlike *aceite* (a kind of ground squirrel). There are only two troubling carnivores on the islands: sand flies (more aptly, sand fleas) and mosquitoes. They are out for blood. You are doubtless experienced with mosquitoes, but the invisible vampires called sand flies (or "no-see-ums" in the native parlance) are the snake in the Caribbean Garden of Eden.

A victim myself, I've learned the virtues of repellent. Ignoring this warning leads to extremely itchy bumps and rashes. Dick Thomas, a veteran of one of the smaller islands, recommends Skintastic and advises ammonia as the best post-bite treatment. (A bath with half a cup of baking soda or oatmeal relieves the itch.)

To that advice I'm going to add more from Bob Schrey. If you spray, don't miss one square inch of exposed skin, and rub the spray in. Spray all edges of your clothing. Wear long sleeves and long pants in early mornings and sunset hours, especially when no breeze is blowing. If the pests begin to get you, flee the flea and go inside. There's no heroism in suicidal stubbornness. It is mainly because of these low-flying bombers that the natives build their beach houses on stilts. A bright note: I am assured by residents

▼▲▼

that almost everyone becomes relatively immune to these micro-vampires after a few weeks or months.

If you are not yet a resident but are simply going on an exploratory trip, make up your own health and medical kit. Since you are going to the tropics, a generous supply of sunscreen (SPF 15 minimal, 25 or higher for children) is mandatory. Sunstroke—usually signaled by fainting, fever, or vomiting—is a real possibility in this area.

Researchers at the Walter Reed Army Institute of Research recently found that when insect repellent was spread on top of sunscreen, the effectiveness of the screen was decreased by more than 40 percent. Even when application of the repellent was delayed for an hour after using sunscreen, there was still a drop of 28 percent in SPF. Reapply the sunscreen often.

A supply of vitamin B—loaded with B_1, B_6, and B_{12}—taken before and during your trip reduces your risk of infection from insect bites. If you expect to spend some time in the Mosquitia, you may wish to take antimalarial pills for two weeks before leaving, during your trip, and for two weeks after. Pack all required medications.

Drinking Water

The warning blared at first-time travelers to the Caribbean area—"Don't drink the water"—is perhaps excessively cautious. After all, in hot climates there is a risk of dehydration. Drink plenty of bottled water, especially after drinking alcohol, another dehydrator.

Still, the warning is sensible. Everyone has heard of Montezuma's revenge, a colorful name for the bouts of diarrhea suffered by pioneering visitors to Mexico who imbibed the local waters. Most American residents restrict themselves to bottled water at first.

Most rural areas and some sections in the cities don't have safe water. In 1997, because the water budget had dried up, 40 percent of the country's water was contaminated. Although in some regions public water does little harm to the locals, remember that the bacteria in Honduras is not the same bacteria you're used to ingesting with impunity at home. Don't drink tap water or use ice cubes made from it. Abstain from raw fruits or vegetables rinsed in tap water, unless they are subsequently peeled.

Many nationals buy water oddly packed in plastic bags. Presumably they too are wary of the public water system, especially where the water has been polluted by chemical runoff from the mining operations. Although the bagged water is cheaper than the bottled, you may be rightly suspicious when you learn that those bags are produced by the same company that makes the insect-killing plastic "raincoats" fitted on the fruit on the banana farms.

The most common symptom of a bacterial invasion is a mild case of diarrhea. If it strikes you, drink plenty of (safe) liquids, avoiding those not bottled, and refrain from dairy products and raw seafood. If the attack lasts more than a few days, seek medical help from a doctor used to treating non-Hondurans.

Most expatriate residents come to accept well and cistern water as safe and will drink the water in hotels and restaurants with filtration

Frank Ford

For high-quality drinking water, visit the restaurant at the Trujillo Bay Hotel. The manager stands out front.

systems warranted safe for the delicate foreign stomach. You surely can trust water served at social occasions by other expatriates. Everywhere else, you should probably carry bottled water.

And Finally . . .

Casual sexual activity is contraindicated. Hondurans were recently shocked when some four thousand cases of AIDS, as well as a number of "old-fashioned" venereal diseases, were discovered within their borders.

One more tip refers to comfort more than to health. One veteran resident confided that she stashes the paper napkins found in restaurants. Traveling frequently around the country, she reports that many otherwise acceptable rest rooms are sadly lacking in toilet paper, and many other rest rooms are sadly lacking. (I have omitted naming her lest, meeting her, you find yourself unable to resist staring at her purse.)

7

▼▲▼▲▼▲▼▲▼▲▼▲▼▲▼▲▼▲▼▲▼▲▼▲▼▲▼▲▼▲▼▲▼

Communication
and Travel

All cities and most towns in Honduras have an office of the government-run Hondutel, at which you can make national and international calls. (Despite rumors you may hear, Hondutel has not been controlled by the military since 1996.)

Once you are living in the country, you'll arrange for your own telephone. Basic service on the mainland costs less than $3 a month.

Don't expect instant installation, especially if you're requesting two or more lines. On Roatán, Gayle Hood reports that she and her husband requested five telephone lines for their realty office. They had to make do with one line for a year and a half. After two years of requests they still have only three.

Honduras now has only two and a half telephones per 100 people, the lowest rate in Central America. But the numbers may soon improve. Hondutel plans to privatize partially, selling 49 percent of the company by the end of 1998. AT&T is one of the likely bidders.

▼▲▼▲▼▲▼▲▼▲▼▲▼▲▼▲▼▲▼▲▼▲▼▲▼▲▼▲▼▲▼▲▼▲▼

In these matters, patience is a needful virtue. Getting "tough" with the phone company will only retard the process. Try a little Caribbean "schmoozing" instead. Sometimes a difficulty that seems unfixable through regular channels will be handled quickly by your maid who has connections with people in the company. Sandra Rensch of Guanaja commends this type of indirect diplomacy. And don't mutter, "Third World!" Many an American impasse is solved obliquely.

While you're awaiting service, you'll find reliable telephone service to the United States, as well as fax and internet access, in the Hondutel offices. You give the number to the clerk, with a deposit to cover the number of minutes you estimate you will need. Most hotels will make calls or set up services for you, usually adding a substantial charge. Some bigger hotels have bilingual stenographers.

Residents of the most remote regions of the Bay Islands do not have phones and communicate by handheld radiophones. San Pedro Sula and Tegucigalpa have coin telephones that take 20 or 50 centavo coins.

If you are in the United States and wish to call Honduras, dial 011, then 504 (Honduras's country code), then the seven-digit local Honduran number. Within Honduras, all except emergency numbers are seven digits. Dial 191 for long distance within Honduras, 192 for information, 198 for fire, and 199 for police.

▼▲▼▲▼▲▼▲▼▲▼▲▼▲▼▲▼

DIALING IN HONDURAS

long distance: 191
information: 192
fire: 198
police: 199

▲▼▲▼▲▼▲▼▲▼▲▼▲▼▲▼▲

From Honduras to anywhere else, simply dial 123 to be connected with the AT&T international operator. You will reach either an operator or a recording. You then supply the area code and number you want, followed by your AT&T calling card number. The cost is reasonable—about $2 per minute from the mainland—unless you are calling collect, in which case you face a $6 surcharge and higher charges per minute. AT&T has most international calls from Honduras sewed up, but punching 121 should put you through to Sprint.

So you don't call the States at an inconvenient hour, remember that the time everywhere in Honduras corresponds with the U.S. Central Time Zone and so is an hour behind the U.S. East Coast and two hours ahead of the West Coast.

Mail

Post offices are open weekdays from 7 a.m. to 6 p.m. and Saturday from 8 a.m. to noon. The efficiency of the postal service varies greatly from place to place. Since it is not altogether reliable, few would entrust checks or important papers to it. Mail from or to the States takes about ten days. For more secure delivery of papers and packages from outside, many residents open private mailboxes at offices in the cities—for example, with Jackson Shipping on Roatán.

UPS, Federal Express, Airborne, and other shippers provide reliable service to Honduras, with UPS favored by Bay Island residents. A letter to or from the States costs about $40 for delivery in one or two business days. If you're sending an important package to the capital, you may do well with courier service. See the phone book in your city.

Electrical Service

Electricity in Honduras is 110 volts, 60 cycles alternating current, the same as in the United States, but cheaper than the States because the source is almost entirely hydroelectric. The usual electric plugs have two undifferentiated blades without the grounding prong, so such plug-ins as electric shavers and hair dryers will fit. A three-prong plug will not fit the outlets, but you can get an adapter at any hardware store. Because a few locales have 220 voltage, it is wise to inquire before connecting.

Air Travel

Efficient and reliable passenger and airfreight services connect Honduras and the American "gateway" cities of Miami, Houston, and New Orleans. Four airlines—TACA, Lacsa, American, and

Continental—bridge the gap on a daily basis. Three more—Iberia, Aero Costa Rica, and Isleña—operate on more limited schedules. Panama's Copa Airlines serves Mexico City. Flights vary as to points of departure and entry, but the Miami to San Pedro Sula run is the most frequent. Presently the round-trip coach fare to and from one of the southern U.S. cities averages $400.

Of the departure cities besides Miami, New York leads in frequency, served by American and Continental daily and by TACA and Lacsa, which alternate daily flights. Dallas and Houston enjoy frequent service, while San Francisco, New Orleans, Los Angeles, and Chicago receive less traffic. In this maze of choices, a knowledgeable travel agent in either country is a godsend. There are no direct flights between Honduras and Canada or Europe.

Between any of the southernmost U.S. cities and Honduras, a direct flight takes just over two hours. American investors have been known to depart from one of the gateway cities, spend an entire day with their interests in Honduras, and be back at their desk in the States the following day.

A billboard encourages Hondurans to protect the river basin at El Cajón, the site of an important hydroelectric project.

Honduras has four international airports. San Pedro Sula has the best. Roatán has rather spartan airport facilities but a well-paved airstrip that easily accommodates 727s and 737s. The runway will probably welcome 757s in the near future. La Ceiba has an ample airfield and a larger terminal building than does Roatán. Tegucigalpa's airstrip is worrisome—too close to the city and uncomfortably short, requiring a steep final descent and a screeching stop. Plans are in the works for relocating it.

Within the country your travel will most often be via the local airlines. The planes are usually safe and reliable twin-prop 18-seaters. Isleña Airlines boasts a perfect safety record. Sosa, Caribbean Air, and Aerohonduras also have good histories, although the FAA does not consider the regional airlines fully up to snuff. One fledgling group, Rolling Airlines, has had two recent accidents.

Flying is often the most comfortable way to travel around Honduras, especially during the rainy season when potholes breed on the roads. Flights are very inexpensive. Presently a flight from Roatán to La Ceiba costs about $25 and a round-trip between La Ceiba and Utila is less than $30. Isleña offers frequent flights between Roatán and Tegucigalpa for about $60. For travel to or from nearby countries, negotiate with the smaller airlines. Copa, Isleña, and Aviateca often offer great bargains, and the larger Lacsa and Taca are not easily underbid.

But be warned: Impatience is ulcerating everywhere, and patience is a virtue especially hallowed in Honduras. The national airlines do not fly at night or in the rain. Since the weather may be fair in your departure city but miserable at your destination, you may find your flight canceled just minutes before departure time. This can be irritating if the only convenient flight dragged you from bed to the airport for an ETD of 6 a.m. (The local airlines love early morning flying conditions.)

Train Travel

Railroads are no help. The few lines are in the north, some 800 miles in all, built by the banana companies to serve themselves.

▼▲▼

There is a line between Tela and San Pedro Sula, but it is slow, dusty, and uncomfortable.

Bus Travel

There are new deluxe buses between La Ceiba, Trujillo, San Pedro Sula, and Tegucigalpa. These are speedy and comfortable, with ample leg and hip room, unlike the buses in the rural areas and smaller cities in which passengers are squeezed five abreast. The new buses have on-board lavatories, taped movies, and refreshments. Service between San Pedro Sula and Tegucigalpa, over about 150 miles of curving highway, takes three hours and costs a little more than $3.

The best way to travel along and near the north coast is on North Coast Shuttle, a minibus service operating from Trujillo and Tela to Tegucigalpa, San Pedro Sula, La Ceiba, and Copán. A speedy and air-conditioned van comes with a bilingual driver, but the scheduled runs are infrequent and much more expensive than buses. Fares range from the one-hour jaunt from Tela to San Pedro Sula for $20 to the all-day trip between Trujillo and Copán for a bit under $60. The shuttle's main office is on Roatán (tel. 552-3202).

Off the main routes, minibuses and vans serve less-traveled areas. Many of the buses are old school buses, retired years ago from their American duties. Generally they are crowded, with small and stiff seats and no racks for luggage. Frequently the overhead is so low that a standing six-footer has to crane his neck. If you are traveling by one of these buses, try to board it at a terminal so as to secure a seat, prefer-ably near the driver. Since there are no bus stops, travelers flag buses from the roadside and pile on like sardines. You can get off anywhere along the road by simply indicating a stopping point to the driver.

Car Travel

A half century ago driving in Honduras was a hair-raising feat for daredevils. Such roads as existed were processions of potholes and mud wallows. You could get to the Pacific from San Pedro Sula but there was no easy way to Tegucigalpa. No passable roads led to the busy Caribbean ports. Ten years later there were still only about 30 miles of paved roads. Today you can drive about two thousand miles on pavement and five times as far on unpaved but hardened all-weather roads. And both kinds are growing. Despite recent "austerity" budgets, Honduras is determinedly spending on its infrastructure. Elsewhere, graded roads are easily navigated in the dry season. Many local roads between pueblos, however, still resemble thrill rides in amusement parks.

The network of paved highways that links the coast, the cities, and some of the towns compares favorably with most of Central America. You can drive on pavement along the Pan American Highway between El Salvador and Nicaragua through Honduras's southern arrowhead, or up to Tegucigalpa and on to San Pedro Sula and Puerto Cortés, west to Copán, or east near the north coast to Tela, La Ceiba, and Trujillo. The road is mostly two-lane but of ample width with generous shoulders. Although the highway is generally well maintained, the driver must nevertheless be vigilant for the potholes and washouts that pock the way, especially after the rainy season. From time to time you'll see speed signs reading 40,

James D. Gollin

Taking taxis is preferable to navigating some Honduran cities by car.

meaning 40 kilometers per hour, but think of them only as caution signs. Nine times out of ten there won't even be need for caution. The sign may have been put up a year before during a bit of repair work and never taken down. No one slows.

Honduras's network of roads is growing constantly, but sign posts are still deficient even on highways, and the unfamiliar driver may stray off course. The turnoff sign you most need may be missing. An unmarked fork may suddenly appear with no sign to indicate which is the highway and which the beginning of a local road that degenerates into a rutted pathway. Advice for male readers: Don't be the butt of female jokes about never asking for directions. Stop and ask from time to time or you may get lost. And slow down for the frequent blind curves on mountain roads. Besides local drivers speeding past you on curves, there is always the possibility of encountering stray cattle and burros.

Importing and Buying Cars

All of this raises a question: Does the foreigner living in Honduras need his own car? The answer is a firm and resounding "It depends." Are you content to remain in one major city with rare excursions into remote parts of the country? Does the apartment you rent or the home you build have a secure and locked garage? (Car theft has become the sport of choice in the cities.) Are you allergic to buses? Do you need the high that many derive from driving? Can you afford to import a car or buy one in the country? Make up your own questions on this matter because the answer lies in that most venerable adage of ancient Greek wisdom, "Know thyself."

If you are applying for a retiree's residency and already own a car in the United States, you can bring it in free of all customs duties. And every five years you can sell your car and bring in another, still duty-free. Of course, you'll have to pay shipping charges of about $600 to get it to Puerto Cortés and another $100 if you choose to settle down on the Bay Islands.

If you are applying for any other residency, importing your own car will cost you at customs: 35 percent on cars and four-door sports vehicles, 15 percent on ordinary vans, and 10 percent on pickups. Heavy trucks pay only 5 percent. Since your auto probably takes only unleaded gas, make sure that fuel is available locally. Your state license or an International Driving License, easily obtainable at your local AAA, allows you to drive legally.

"If you are applying for a retiree's residency and already own a car in the United States, you can bring it in free of all customs duties."

What if you don't have a car but think you'll want one in Honduras? First, get your Honduran driver's license—essentially an eye exam costing $15. For a vehicle, consider going to San Pedro Sula and browsing for used cars. One option is purchasing a new Russian-made UAZ Jeep—built like a tank, simple in design, and easy to maintain—for about $12,000. I admire the popular four-door Toyota pickups, but they carry stickers that translate close to $30,000. In these and in the most frequently rented cars you'll need to be able to handle manual gearshifts.

Renting a Car

Rentals make sense for round-trip sightseeing excursions from a city into the surrounding countryside, but they can be an expensive way to travel from one city to another. Rental agencies in Honduras do not allow the convenience of renting in one city and dropping off the car in another. You will have to pay a driver's fee—ranging from $25 to $60—for the return of the car to the original renting office. For such trips, new buses or the regional airlines are much more economical.

Renting a car occasionally can be a sensible option on the mainland. Rental cars are available and generally well maintained. There are rental offices in all airports and in the centers of major cities. Besides well-known names like Toyota, Budget, and Avis—the last, I am told, not under the jurisdiction of its U.S. counterpart—there are local companies like Maya Rent-a-Car that frequently undercut their competitors. Rates tend to be a little higher than in the States: about $50 to $75 per day for passenger cars and about $55 for a four-door Toyota pickup.

Take the time to learn and understand all the conditions of rental. Most agreements bar you from taking the vehicle out of the country. Some outfits allow you only 150 free kilometers (just under 100 miles) before imposing substantial charges for extra distances. No insurance is required.

Good regional maps can be purchased from the omnipresent Texaco stations, where a gallon of unleaded gas costs just under $2. Pumps sometimes display liters (about 3.8 liters per gallon), and some of them were calibrated before inflation, so that they register only half the accurate price. If you stop at a station and are told to "pay double" (*paga doble*), do so. You are not being cheated.

Supergasoline (leaded) costs about $1.75 per gallon. Unleaded did not go on sale until December 1995. A dawning awareness of the possibility of air pollution in the cities finally forced the change. ESSO offers unleaded gas at three stations in Tegucigalpa. Texaco, as noted above, also has this option, as does Shell on Roatán. Leaded regular suits most rental cars at a cost of about 5 cents less per gallon, but be sure to ask the rental agency which variety of fuel your car requires.

On Roatán you can rent a pickup for $46 per day and a four-wheel drive for about $15 more. They're very practical if you're exploring the rough roads of the East End. For any trips west of Coxen Hole, engage a taxi. On Guanaja you can't rent a car for there is only one road, the length of a short walk. Here, motor boats are the touring vehicle of choice: Renting one with a driver cost me about $30 an hour. On Utila walk or rent a bike unless you want to see property on the other side of the lagoon, in which case you'll need a boat.

Taxis

Do not rent a car to see a city that you are visiting. A rented car in the cities can be very frustrating, especially in the maze that is downtown Tegucigalpa. Take taxis instead. That advice may sound extravagant to those used to the "arm-and-a-leg" fares in North America or Europe, but taxi travel in Honduras is surprisingly affordable. Most cabs are small Japanese models, easy on gas, and the labor cost is low. A trip of several miles within a city will seldom cost more than a dollar or two.

The fare, however, is always negotiated before starting. Honduran taxis don't have meters. Tell the driver your destination and ask his price. If you don't speak Spanish, have a small pad with you and print the address so that he understands and can write the fare. If it is much more than your hotel clerk suggested, for example, hail another cab. Upon arrival, have the exact amount ready and hand it over without any tip unless the driver has done some unusual favor for you or carried your luggage. Honduran nationals are very stern when instructing gringos in this aspect of taxi etiquette. Apparently they don't wish to see cabbies presuming an epidemic of automatic tipping.

If you need to make several short stops in succession, you can usually agree on a modest hourly rate for a taxi. A half-day excursion by cab to nearby towns and villages will be cheaper and easier than renting a car for the day.

8

▾▲▾

¿Se Habla Español?

This chapter is intended for readers who don't speak Spanish fluently. Those who do should either skim or skip it. If you plan to visit only the Bay Islands, or if you sign up for a tour with English-speaking guides, then English will suffice in Honduras. If you have devised a tour of your own making, you'll have no need of Spanish if you confine your visits to the relatively expensive tourist hotels in the large cities. The managers and at least one desk clerk will speak fluent English and most bellhops will know at least a smattering.

Just about every islander on Roatán speaks English, and most consider themselves English. On Guanaja the expatriate residents you may visit and the staff of the dive shops and hotels like the Posada del Sol will speak English. But in the town of Guanaja, known by the locals as Bonacca or El Cayo, the "Venice of Honduras," you will probably need at least a basic Spanish vocabulary. The same generalization applies to Utila. Although you'll hear English spoken there, in some of the businesses and cafés on the main street you may find yourself buying or ordering with the aid of a phrase book. The Berlitz *Latin-American Spanish Phrase Book and Dictionary* is an inexpensive pocket-size companion. A few hours spent perusing it before leaving or in flight will pay off, especially if a Spanish speaker has gotten you started on your vowels and consonants.

On the mainland, if you intend to stay only in large tourist hotels in the larger cities, you will manage very well within your accommodations. Once outside, however, you will find that the national language is indeed Spanish. A basic knowledge of the language such as offered by your phrase book will do for most simple transactions. The Spanish-speaking citizens know that Americans are not linguists. An old joke defines a person with three languages as "trilingual," one with two languages as "bilingual," and one with only one language as "gring-al."

At first the Spanish replies to your faltering questions and statements will run over you like an express train. Even if you know some of the words, you'll probably be left far behind in the translation. But if you pepper your *despacios* and *lentamentes* with a generous number of *por favors*, you will find that most mainlanders will not only slow down but even substitute synonyms for Spanish words you clearly don't understand.

Unlike the French, Central Americans are not fixated on purity of language and will bear patiently the most egregious errors with only a quickly suppressed smile. Long used to the intrusion of foreigners on their turf, they have become linguistically imaginative and adept at gesticulating helpfully when gaps occur.

LANGUAGE SCHOOLS IN HONDURAS

Copán Ruinas:	Ixbalanque Spanish School, 651-4432
Trujillo:	Ixbalanque Escuela de Español, 434-4461
	Centro Internacional de Idiomas, 434-4777
La Ceiba:	Eco-Escuela de Español, 443-2762
Tegucigalpa:	Centro Cultural Alemán, 237-1555

When gaps do occur, if you can't find the Spanish word you need, try pronouncing the English counterpart as if it were Spanish, perhaps adding a final vowel. Because of the Latin roots in their ancestry, nearly three thousand words are almost identical in both tongues. There's a good chance the trick will work—especially if the English word ends in *sion, tion, ant, ent, or ence,* or if it belongs to technical or mechanical nomenclature. If the term is scientific, artistic, or philosophic, because often classical Greek in origin, it commonly has near twins in both languages.

Pronunciation

Because Spanish is a phonetic language, learning to pronounce it is surprisingly easy. To acquire an authentic accent may take years, but Hondurans are willing to settle for merely understandable diction. Central American Spanish is fairly uniform, but there are some differences between countries in the treatment of some combinations like *ll* and *ch*, and even single consonants like *j* and *x*.

In words ending with a vowel, or *n* or *s*, the next to last syllable is stressed. So *techo* is "TAY-cho" and *silla* is "SEE-yah." *Gracias* is "GRAH-syas" and *joven* is "KHO-behn." In that last word, I should explain that Central Americans understand the letter *v* when they hear it but usually pronounce it like a *b*. In words ending with a consonant, except *n* or *s*, hit the last syllable. *Ferrocarril* is "feh-ro-kah-REEL" and *cerrar* is "seh-RAHR." Words that depart from those rules of accent have an acute accent over the exceptional syllable. So *también* is "tam-BYAYN" and *rincón* is "reen-KOHN."

If you learned some Spanish in school, unlearn any Castilian *ll*: Central Americans omit any *l* sound from the double *l*. In addition, Hondurans pronounce *s* or soft *c* like our English *s*, refraining from the Castilian lisp.

Learning Conversational Spanish

If you completed your first tour of Honduras with little or no Spanish, you may feel self-congratulatory, but chances are you wished you knew more of the language. But what if, after that initial tour, you fall in love with the country and determine to stay on extended visas or apply for residence? Unless you plan to confine your socializing to hotel desk clerks, you had better acquire a fair ability in the language, something more than the kitchen or restaurant Spanish you have already picked up from small phrase books or handheld translating computers.

Spanish 101

In your primary stages of attempting Spanish, it's good to familiarize yourself with four situations:

Referring to Yourself: You may be asked your nationality. If you're from the United States, please do not answer "American" or even "North American." The latter expression disregards Canada and the former denies that the Honduran speaking to you is in the same hemisphere. Please say "United States" or, if you are trying out your Spanish, "*Yo soy estadounidense*"—"I'm a United Stateser." (The term *gringo* in Honduras is usually no more than a shorthand identification of American, said without the disparaging tone common in much of Central America. The origin of the term is uncertain. One version imagines the Philippine Islanders saying to Teddy Roosevelt's green-uniformed Rough Riders, "Greens, go home.")

Referring to Honduran Citizens: Referring to the culture of the country, especially of the mainland, use Ladino, not Latino. The *d* is a reminder of the Amerindian heritage, part of the

True, in the four largest cities you will find many English speakers including bilingual native Hondurans, but you will not enjoy the richness of the country if you confine yourself to frequent phrases and insist on oversimplified responses. Perfection in syntax is not a requisite. Your aim is conversational ease and an extensive vocabulary.

For courses in conversational Spanish, check your local

mestizo culture. And speaking of mainland citizens, call them "*nacionales*" in Spanish and "nationals" in English. *Nativos* (natives) is not used. *Aborigenes* describes the government-sheltered pure-blooded Amerindians.

Addressing Individuals: Suppose a man's calling card reads Luis Jorge Garcia Lopez. The last two names may have a connective *y* (and) or they may not. He is a stranger and you will address him as Señor, but which name should you use?

The answer is Garcia. The final name in the group is his mother's family name. Once married, his wife, formerly perhaps Angela Maria Suarez y Ortiz, drops her matrilineal name, adds her husband's name, and becomes Angela Maria Suarez de Garcia. She is formally addressed as Señora Garcia.

Finding Addresses: 18 Concordia Street is written as Calle Concordia 18. Fifth Avenue is 5ª Avenida, with the superscript equivalent to our *th* in 5th. Sometimes a location is designated by its neighorhood, called *barrio* and abbreviated Bo. So too a district may be named a *colonia* and shortened to Col.

resources. (The average high school course will not do. You want the spoken word, not grammar or orthography.) Libraries and nearby colleges with adult education divisions are a possibility. Ransack your library for conversation books written in dialog form—*Entre Tú y Yo,* for instance.

You might consider hiring a tutor. That sounds expensive, but it can be economical and fruitful. A local teacher or, cheaper still, a bilingual college student with some teaching experience may set very reasonable rates.

The government has developed some splendid audiocassettes. There are also well-known tape courses like Linguaphone, Audio-Forum, and Spoken Language Services. Cassettes and compact discs let you listen while driving or exercising. Multimedia programs are produced by Berlitz, Barron's, Living Language, NTC Publishing, and Penton Overseas. Look in computer software and travel shops. Living Language offers CD-ROMs that even check your accent. Finally, there are over two hundred Berlitz Language Centers with a long menu of options from relatively inexpensive group courses to very expensive tutorials called "total immersion."

Learning from the Locals

Best of all, learn the language in Honduras. There you will put your lessons to daily use, and your articulation, accent, and usage will be appropriate to the native practice. Every country modifies its language to suit itself, and therefore your final school of Honduran Spanish will be Honduras. Whatever Spanish you now possess may differ slightly in accent, pronunciation, and rhythm. Don't worry about it. People will welcome your attempts in the language and reach out to help.

Local usage often does vary from textbooks and dictionaries. For example, you have probably learned from texts that *tú* is the form used when speaking to family members and close friends rather than the formal *usted.* But in Honduras you will usually hear *vos* instead of *tú.* Some seniors may still use *tú,* but most Hondurans resist the form as old-fashioned, condescending, and a bit pretentious.

Dictionaries define *recto* as "straight, a straight line." The first time I rented a car in the country and asked for directions, I was told "*recto, recto, recto*," always three times. (In other countries the favored word is *derecho*, but not in Honduras.) But as soon as I got on the highway, I found that no road in that mountainous terrain was straight. I finally decided that *recto* really means something like "Follow the highway and don't allow yourself to be seduced by other roads, however attractive they may seem."

Misunderstandings Will Happen

Ever since the Tower of Babel there has been confusion of tongues. Marietta Linton, mother of Trujillo's language school director, tells about an American relative some years ago who was picked up by the police on a mistaken identity matter. At his urging—in Spanish, for they had no English—they drove past his brother's

At Belinda Linton's language school in Trujillo, students work in small groups inside these breezy classrooms.

house and allowed him a moment to call in the open door for help. He had only time to shout, "Help! The police are taking me to the cooler!" The mood in the police car instantly darkened, and the bewildered American found himself roughly hurled into a cell and kept incommunicado overnight. This puzzling hostility was cleared up the following day when his brother announced that a charge had been lodged of using obscene and abusive language to describe an officer of the law. The policemen thought they were hearing gringo-garbled Spanish and were sure that they heard two words: *policia* and *culo*. The meaning they took from that—translated into vulgar modern lingo—was "This cop is an asshole." The Bostonian's suppression of the *r* in the slangy "cooler" contributed to the misunderstanding.

Widely differing backgrounds can also cause strange impasses, especially with Honduran servants. Many housemaids are illiterate, so you cannot with any assurance spell names over the telephone. Nonetheless, they have good memories and retain any reminders you give them. I once called Marietta Linton and the maid told me she was out. I asked her to say that Señor Ford had called. "Ford," I said, "As in the car." The memo Marietta received was "A Señor Bush called, as in the car." How Bush got into the chain we couldn't figure, until a friend reminded me of Pablo Bush. Don Pablo, now about 90, once a pioneer explorer of Mayan ruins in the Yucatán, has operated the exclusive Ford agency in Mexico—and in all Central America as far as I know—and to the maid, "Bush" was the equivalent of "Ford."

According to Maureen Robinson, translator and expatriate resident of San Pedro Sula, Europeans adapt better to Honduras, mostly because they are more willing to really learn Spanish, whereas Americans "spend a lot of time trying to find themselves and one another." For example, instead of joining the International Women's Club, American women are more likely to form an English-speaking women's club of their own. Even on Roatán, English-speaking women remain somewhat separate. Americans, Maureen concludes, would gain more acceptance by keeping a lower national profile and by "blending" more. And blending is best done by sharing a language.

Justly or unjustly, as a group we Americans are considered very unmannerly by most of the world. But frequent use of formal courtesies can help us shed the "ugly American" label. In Honduras, it is almost impossible to be excessive in the use of *gracias*, *por favor*, *señor*, *señora*, and the like. These words will ease your way wonderfully.

9

▼▲▼▲▼▲▼▲▼▲▼▲▼▲▼▲▼▲▼▲▼▲▼▲▼▲▼▲▼▲▼▲▼▲▼▲▼▲▼

Prime Living Choices

T his chapter describes a dozen places in Honduras where you will find delightful living. Obviously I cannot choose for you, but I have tried to include in each description enough advantages and drawbacks to enable you to make preliminary guesses as to which will best suit your tastes, preferences, personality, and finances. Please remember an extended visit should precede any purchase.

The Bay Islands (Islas de la Bahía)

"Much have I traveled in realms of gold," boasted John Keats. He was singing the praises of literature, but the phrase aptly describes the dazzling beaches that gird the Bay Islands and the North Coast.

If you took your first trip mostly as a vacation jaunt, chances are your first stop was the Bay Islands and you landed on the island that has an international airport, the largest island, Roatán. Your first sight of it from the air probably reawakened that old dream of a sun-blessed Eden.

▼▲▼▲▼▲▼▲▼▲▼▲▼▲▼▲▼▲▼▲▼▲▼▲▼▲▼▲▼▲▼▲▼▲▼▲▼

Although Honduras, despite its recent efforts at publicizing its attractions, remains a secret eluding most travel agencies, Roatán and two of its sister islands have become fairly well known among scuba diving fans. Sports fishermen and snorkelers are almost equally enthusiastic.

The Bay Islands include eight islands and 65 cays with a total land area of 238 square kilometers (about 92 square miles), situated between 22 and 38 miles from the north coast. The three largest and most visited form an arc tilted to the northeast with Utila, the closest north of La Ceiba, then Roatán, the largest, and Guanaja, above Trujillo. Three much smaller islands, accessible only by boat, Helene, Morat, and Barbareta, are strung out between Roatán and Guanaja. The tiny Cayos Cochinos (Hog Isles) are closer to La Ceiba. They are the tips of submerged mountains extending from

▼▲▼▲▼▲▼▲▼▲▼▲▼▲▼▲▼▲▼▲▼▲▼▲▼▲▼▲▼▲▼▲▼▲▼▲▼

TOUR COMPANIES

IN THE UNITED STATES:
American Tours and Travel (206) 623-8850
Discovery Tours (800) 926-6575 or (561) 243-6276
Great Trips (800) 552-3419
Honduras Travel (212) 972-6867
Roatán Charters (800) 282-8932
Visit Central America Program (800) 255-8222

IN HONDURAS:
Ecohonduras (443-0933)
Euro Honduras (443-0933)
Explore Honduras (552-6239)
Garifuna Tours (448-2904)
Hondu Maya (558-1059)
La Moskitia Ecoaventuras (237-9398)
Mayan VIP Tours (553-4672)
MC Tours (553-3076)
Ríos Honduras/Caribbean Travel Agency (443-0780)

▲▼▲▼▲▼▲▼▲▼▲▼▲▼▲▼▲▼▲▼▲▼▲▼▲▼▲▼▲▼▲▼▲▼▲▼▲

the mainland's Omoa chain—the highest peak a bit less than 1,400 feet above water—and have sweeping rises and long sloping valleys. For the purposes of a first trip, I will discuss only the three largest islands, the ones most people mean when mentioning the Bay Islands.

These islands are major contributors to Honduras's cultural and ethnic diversity. The islanders are a mix of white, black, and mulatto peoples, descended from English-speaking whites and blacks who came in the mid-nineteenth century from Belize, when it was British Honduras, and from the Cayman Islands.

This small group, probably fewer than 25,000, still speaks an English flavored with Creole and follows customs akin to those of the West Indies. Demographers describe their culture as Anglo-Afro-Antillean Caribbean. Some inhabitants even claim descent from the English pirates who used to find safe harbor there, following channels through the encircling reefs into sheltering bays where the heavier Spanish warships could not follow. Names like Jones, Smith, and White are common. The prevailing religious

James D. Gollin

Roatán is the largest of the Bay Islands—and the most popular.

affiliation is not Catholic but Protestant, mostly Methodist. Traces of the aboriginal Paya Indian culture add to the mix.

So distinct from the mainland are these islands that the inhabitants don't speak of traveling to the "mainland" but of going to "Honduras." Nor do the mainlanders usually think of the inhabitants as country-men; they call them "islanders" or "the English" (*ingleses*).

A 1980 estimate classified them as 42 percent black, 27 percent white, and 16 percent "colored," meaning mixed white and black, not to be confused with the mestizos. Another 4 percent of the popula-tion are descendants of Carib Indians and shipwrecked African slaves: the Garifunas, or Black Caribs, who have clung to Roatán despite Spanish resettlement programs, and who maintain a 200-year-old settlement on the north shore at Punta Gorda. An easy sociability prevails on the islands, as does a general sense of social equality. No one I've talked to reports any trace of racism.

In the last quarter century, hundreds of North American and European expatriates have taken up residence throughout the islands. The rest of the inhabitants are Ladinos, sent from the main-land mostly for the customs and administrative work required of the tourism industry. Many of them speak only Spanish, a major social barrier until the local public schools began teaching in Spanish and the private schools became bilingual.

Now most islanders speak at least some *Español*, yet they fre-quently refer guardedly to the newcomers as "the Spanish" and feel that these migrants are changing the local culture. Such ill feelings seem not to be based on racial grounds but instead as hostility against outsiders. One crusty old Briton described Roatán as "Paradise except for the damned government."

Roatán

If diving is on your wish list, and sunbathing and aquatic sports are your favorites, you've certainly come to the right place. Roatán is embraced by crystalline waters with a year-round average tempera-ture a notch or two above or below 80 degrees. The marvelous fring-ing coral reefs keep the sea serene, especially from the middle of February to early September.

You'll find almost every type of Caribbean coral and sponge, as well as rainbows of animals ranging from parrot fish and sea horses to the more somber sea turtles, manta rays, and, every once in a while, herbivorous (thankfully!) whale sharks.

Sheer walls of coral start at only 20 feet below the surface. Two large wrecks, both of which are frequented by divers, are visible off the coasts of Roatán and Guanaja. The eastern Oak Ridge as well as the West End are often praised for their diving sites, but shore diving and snorkeling can be equally rewarding. Many great sites are only minutes from hotels.

If you decide to reside here and are not too sedentary, importing your own car can make sense. There is a good road running almost the entire length of the 25-mile-long island. It's paved from Coxen Hole north to Sandy Bay and then west through Anthony's Cay and Half Moon Bay to West End, with good dirt spurs to Flowers Bay, West Bay Beach, and Watering Place. Driving east, the pavement continues a few miles beyond French Harbor. The dirt road that continues to Camp Bay Beach is graded and well kept, especially

The Bay Islands are a diver's paradise.

James D. Gollin

from Easter until the October rains (there is a great processional move to the eastern end for Easter Sunday). Branch roads will take you to Punta Gorda or Oak Ridge.

The eastern tip of the island, along with Barbareta and Morat—where you will find mangroves, coral reefs, and tropical rain forest—is protected as Barbareta Marine National Park. (The status of Morat Island has needed clarification since it was sold to a non-Honduran in the late 1980s. Roatán's court recently ruled the sale void under Article 107 of the constitution, allowing only Hondurans by birth to purchase any island or cay. That decision is under appeal.) At the other end of the island, Sandy Bay and West End Marine Park are also protected.

Everywhere there are public beaches of white sand and shading palm, sea grape, and breadfruit trees. So fertile is the land and so fertilizing the sun that private lots are divided by "living fences," wooden posts metamorphosed into trees with a kaleidoscope of flowering plants in relatively straight lines. Orchids spliced onto palm trees grow in profusion.

Some beaches, especially near Oak Ridge and Port Royal, seem almost deserted. There are no lifeguards, so prudent residents bathe in each other's company, despite the lack of surf. They also resist napping under the palm trees, as coconuts fall with a vengeance.

If you buy beachfront property here, the south side is breezier. However, the hills on either side usually offer cooling winds. The trade winds on the south side hold down the insects, while the West End, although beautiful, can be rather buggy.

But whether buying property here, on the other islands, or on the coast, don't imagine that your ownership is without let or stay. All beaches are public, and the mangroves that partly obscure your view may not be cut down—they're protected by law. Nor may you build a multistory house: Buildings may not be taller than the loftiest palm tree.

The retiree with a very modest income and a small nest egg may find this pleasure spot a financial strain, especially in the overdeveloped West End. An income of at least $1,000 per month per person and at least $50,000 under the mattress is necessary if you seriously hope to build and keep a home anywhere on Roatán, and even then you must calculate carefully.

However, Bob Schrey, a local Realtor, feels that there are still bargains to be found. Advertising and publicity, he says, go to high-profile projects priced in the hundreds of thousands, but lots of properties can be bought for much less.

And good inexpensive rentals often reward a persistent search. He and his wife rent a 700-square-foot wooden house one block from the beach in a grove of palm and banana trees. Raised about 12 feet off the ground, the house has good decks, ceiling fans, and louvered windows, which make air conditioning unnecessary. (The owner of their house, a very handy type, built it himself for $10,000.)

Construction with treated wood on the islands costs about $30 or $35 per square foot; concrete-block construction costs almost twice that. Honduras's skilled wood craftsmen can fill in the gaps in your furnishings, from eight-foot-tall mahogany wardrobes to doors with Mayan monkey gods.

Grocery shopping on Roatán is easy. There is a native market at Coxen Hole and a big one at French Harbor, a few miles along the road to the east. The latter, an open-air Spanish-style municipal market, has stalls that at first can be noisy and confusing to the inexperienced gringo. The island's larger supermarket, Eldon's, also at French Harbor, doubles as a Shell gas station and is closed on Saturday to observe the Seventh-Day Sabbath. Warren's in Coxen Hole is the other supermarket. In the West End, a smaller store with the proud title Super Tienda Chris offers excellent telephone and fax services at better rates than any of the hotels.

In the Caribbean the transition from a polychrome sunset to dark is dramatically abrupt: There is almost no dusk. Evenings on the islands tend to be slow and quiet, and socializing over dinner and drinks is the general rule. If after all the excitement you find you're not ready for sleep, a hammock on your deck fanned by the trade winds under a canopy of stars is a sure cure for insomnia.

There is no movie house on any of the islands, though one company does provide cable TV. Many hotels have TV lounges; a few use projection TV to air six-month-old films in English with Spanish subtitles. Each night at about seven, the Bamboo Hut in West End dedicates its barroom to this purpose. On Monday night the Sueño del Mar Hotel does the same. If you "gotta dance," Celebrity in French Harbor offers reggae and salsa. Nearby is Bolongos, patronized by the locals. Harbor View in Coxen Hole is cheaper and noisier. All have small cover charges of $1 or $2.

Daytime entertainment depends on one's initiative and imagination. Aquatic sports are obviously favored. An enjoyable family outing is snorkeling at the beautiful West Bay Beach. At present Roatán offers no golf, bowling, or films, and, other than the archaeologically oriented Roatán Museum, you will find few cultural attractions.

Despite the greater expense of living on Roatán, residents with young children often prefer this island and the safe, tranquil life it allows. Holly Canale of RE/MAX Realty feels the Bay Islands are better for raising kids than Costa Rica and Belize. "There is a simplicity of lifestyle here and the absorption of different cultures with not a trace of racism," she says.

If you have young children and see yourself moving to Roatán as an investor resident rather than a retiree, you will naturally be concerned about your children's education. If your children only speak English they'll have to attend bilingual private schools. With rare exceptions, the public schools are widely considered inferior. The private schools are not segregated; many nationals who can afford them send their children there, too.

There are five private schools for girls and seven for boys, ranging from preschool through tenth grade. They cost $60 per month ($40 for preschool), considerably more than private schools on the mainland. Most schools are run by local churches.

Guanaja

When first sighted from the air, it is clear that this island is the upper ridge of an otherwise submerged mountain. Rising as high as 1,400 feet, the land reaches a stratospheric altitude by Bay Island standards. Seemingly without a road, green and lushly forested, and crowned by a tiara of pine trees (Columbus called it Pine Island), this 12- by 4-mile marine jewel offers unspoiled beauty, superb waterfalls, and gorgeous sunsets. And the diving is exceptional. In fact, the wall off Mango Bight provides some of the best diving in the world.

Honduran officialdom calls the capital town Guanaja, but the natives call it Bonacca or El Cayo (the Key or Islet). It is an island in itself, a watery key just off the coast. About 5,000 inhabitants crowd the small town, roughly 80 percent of the total population of the island. Savannah Bight is next in number of inhabitants; Mango Bight, third.

A political center crisscrossed by canals with wooden walkways and narrow lanes devoid of cars, Bonacca has been fancifully labeled "the Venice of the Caribbean." But other than the trash in the canals and the absence of cars, you won't find much here to remind you of Venice, and I doubt that many Americans would choose to retire here.

Instead, a scattering of friendly expatriates, mostly retirees, luxuriate in the virtually undiscovered green slopes of the main island amid waterfalls, breathtaking views, white-sand beaches, and blankets of wild fruit trees and flowers. Most of them have built their own homes, including three estates belonging to internationally known figures. Others are buying homes in new developments. Most of the houses are wooden, but now there are two concrete mixers on the island, so concrete-block construction fronted with stucco is becoming more common.

Retirees note a strong sense of belonging here, even though neighbors are often at a distance. Emotional support is not lacking. When one longtime expatriate couple returned to the States for medical reasons, 300 people, most of them natives, turned out to give them a farewell send-off, showering them with presents.

James D. Gollin

Fewer expats choose tiny Guanaja.

▼▲▼

American holidays don't pass unnoticed either. Locals and gringos join forces for a big celebration on July 4. "The gringos are part of our life," says Kenya Lima de Zapata—the Department of Tourism's *jefe regional* of the Bay Islands. "What are we looking for? Sustainable development, not a tourist boom. Growth must accord with ecological preservation. We are determined not to repeat others' mistakes like the boom of Miami and the abuses of Bermuda."

"There is a parallel but also a difference between Roatán and Guanaja," observes Julius Rensch, a retired American audiologist and longtime resident of Guanaja. "Roatán is more sophisticated with the influx of legions of tourists thanks to its jet port which international passengers use as an entry to Honduras. Because tourists can only come to Guanaja by small planes and go a bit out of the way to visit us, the smaller numbers that do come are usually more discriminating and interesting. That description carries over to those who settle here."

"New residents need not be well-to-do. We were never wealthy," adds Rensch. "A retiree without small children and with a modest income—pension and/or Social Security—and a stockpile of, say, $40,000 is an ideal resident. The small investor-resident also has a good chance if he comes here as a good neighbor. There is always something we need. I see this as a nation on the brink of something great. Honduras is growing in a positive way."

Dr. Michael Cooper, a British retiree, has also noted a difference between the two islands. "I like Roatán, but it's more commercial," he says. "There's more riffraff, more thievery. Tourism here on Guanaja is no automatic reflex, and what tourism we get attracts more self-sufficient types. . . . They're not layabouts waiting for service."

There are garden spots available here for the most discriminating shopper. High up on the hill there are secluded areas where an acre of land can be purchased for about $500. Down on the waterfront a typical developed (that is, with all utilities and an access road) 300-by 100-foot lot will run about $35,000. In between the two extremes are lots with in-between prices, but anything off the beach will necessitate carving a path to the shoreline. Because building materials are shipped in LST-type boats, construction costs are similar to those on Roatán—higher than on the mainland.

According to *International Living*, U.S. citizens have been involved in at least 60 property disputes in Honduras. Clear title to purchased land is particularly a problem in Guanaja because old deeds are vague, measurements inexact, and registration faulty. Some Realtors are suspected of peddling land with very dubious titles.

Municipalities have also made mistakes. Empowered in 1991 to sell some national land, officials sometimes assumed property lying unused was "national" and so would sell a parcel—whereupon an outraged owner would show up bearing his copy of an ancient original deed. Jack Midence, engineer, surveyor, and developer of 15 acres in Sandy Bight, blames the problem on inexact surveys in the old days. Deeds might be as vague as "five acres in Mango Bight," and often lacked any indication of boundaries.

Midence stresses the importance of using a Realtor to find property, a diligent notary to search the title, a capable surveyor to draw the lines, and a reputable lawyer to register and protect your claim. You must go beyond your Realtor's assurances of safety and search the title as far back as possible—"Back to the Queen," says Kenya. And the queen she has in mind is Victoria.

Although you can get direct connections to Bonacca for electricity and water, water can be a problem. In 1995 scanty rainfall left even Bonacca running low. Some residents built cisterns, an expensive but reliable measure.

Power comes from Bonacca via underwater cable. Some residents use batteries or small generators as backups. Midence has put in a device that converts from 12 volts DC to 120 AC and vice versa. When the power is on, it charges heavy-duty truck-type batteries. When the power is off, it automatically switches to the batteries. Alternatively, the system can be hooked up to solar panels or a windmill. Wind is a reliable constant on Guanaja, and the sun shines benignly on all three islands.

There is one road on the island—from Savannah Bight to where the airport used to be at Mango Bight—and it will probably remain the only one. It would be folly to build more roads on Guanaja. Any road would have to follow the ridge. Keeping it under a 25 percent grade and making practicable descents to the shoreline would be

Herculean. Dr. Cooper dreams of clearing paths to friends' houses that a golf cart might manage, but he agrees with the other residents that no real road is wanted or needed.

Clearly the residents have no use for the family car. On this island the indispensable vehicle is a motorboat. Of course, some use sailboats—usually sloops and ketches—for fishing, but for rapid transport to neighbors' homes miles away, and for transport to the Bonacca and the other Bay Islands, a motorboat is a necessity.

Utila

The mile-long main street, lined with modest Victorian houses and picket fences, unassuming lodgings, dive shops, convenience stores, bike rental shops, and simple restaurants, will make clear to you why residents of the two larger islands complain that Utila has gone "on the cheap." It is true that it attracts a disproportionate number of backpackers and diving enthusiasts with limited funds. But it has that small-town ease and friendliness that Americans long for. This is a good place to relax.

Most of the people here speak English. The first major non-aboriginal group to settle Utila was a band of white Cayman Islanders fleeing their homeland in the 1830s. They tended to inter-marry—some say there was an imprudent number of second-cousin unions—and today there are a number of fair-skinned inhabitants who practice an almost British politeness.

Of the 60 or so foreigners living on Utila, perhaps a third are young diving instructors. As one resident described the population, "People here show true Honduran charm. They don't carry an atti-tude like Bahamans and Jamaicans." Not much here is "touristy." Captain Ron, a fisherman's outfitter connected with the Utila Lodge, says he prefers Utila to Roatán because "Here people take time. It's less pressured and Americanized."

It is certainly laid back, and Americans who settle here do so for precisely that atmosphere. The island can make you feel as though you've stepped onto an old movie set—a romantic comedy set in a small Louisiana town at the beginning of the twentieth century.

Banking, mail, and telephone services are adequate, but health facilities are not as reliable. The Community Clinic fronts the park, but a physician's assistant is in charge and antibiotics and Valium seem to be the invariable treatments. As elsewhere on the Bay Islands, the advice remains the same: If you are sick, head for the mainland.

Electrification on Utila is somewhat sporadic. A large-scale electrification project that started in Guanaja was supposed to reach Utila, but funds ran short. The World Bank may have remedied this problem by the time you read this, but for now residents must be content with what they have. Town lights and power go off at midnight, and you'll need a flashlight for nocturnal bathroom visits in most guest houses. Some American residents install a generator for late-night needs and as backup for computers and other electrical equipment.

Modest but acceptable two-bedroom houses with air conditioning can be found on the island for about $25,000. Larger houses are available for $40,000. A four-bedroom, one-bath house in East Harbor, facing the ocean, with two 30-foot boat slips, a sundeck, air conditioning, cable TV, and telephone was discovered by *International Living* scouts for $80,000. The property taxes on these three homes range between $25 and $100 per year.

Although entertainment is limited, Utila possesses the nearest thing to a movie house on the Bay Islands. The Utila Film Club shows fairly recent videos in a room capable of seating 30 people on metal folding chairs. There are also a few popular bars attached to restaurants and one disco, as Honduran dance spots are called.

If you prefer to get your entertainment fix during the day, you can go deep-sea fishing for sailfish, albacore, or mackerel. But get a fishing license first.

La Ceiba

The cheerful city of La Ceiba (pronounced SAY-bah) is a welcoming doorway to mainland Honduras. Despite being the third largest city in Honduras with a population of 60,000, La Ceiba has a pleasant small-town feeling and is easy to get to know, especially the central area with its grid of paved streets and avenues. The city derives its name from the huge and ancient ceiba trees, shaped like umbrellas, which once shaded its embryonic trade center and still defy age, standing tall on the western bank of the estuary running south from the sea and ending near the soccer stadium.

The umbrella shape is appropriate, for the cities of the North Coast receive an extra dividend of rain. Even so, a brightness persists in the air, and usually the sun is quick to return. (I say usually because in 1994 the heavens dumped 22 inches on La Ceiba in five days.)

Because it is flat and coastal, the city is hot, but a welcome breeze usually wafts off the harbor in the afternoon and evening. The otherwise level horizon is pierced to the south by the towering Pico Bonito, an 8,500-foot representative of the Nombre de Dios range.

It was here that Standard Fruit (Dole) developed the giant disease-resistant Cavendish banana after early varieties of banana fell victim to "Panama disease" in the 1930s. Dole banana and

NOT TO SCALE

pineapple shipments continue to keep the port bustling but no longer do so exclusively. Other industries have been burgeoning in this "free zone" thanks to government dispensations from taxes.

If you arrive in the middle of May, you'll witness the exuberant *carnaval*, a kind of Caribbean Mardi Gras without Lent. The week of celebration honors patron saint Isidro with marches, fantastic costumes, floats, dancing, and general good-natured hoopla. But that spirit of celebration seems to cling after the beauty queens hang up their gowns and return the costume jewelry. As Hondurans say, "La Ceiba is always a festival. Tegucigalpa is our political capital, San Pedro our business capital, and La Ceiba our fun capital." Noted for its hospitality and warmth, La Ceiba is also an important commercial center.

Almost anything you buy here will be at least 20 percent cheaper than on the islands. Oceanview lots, a bit under an acre, start as low as $5,500. It is possible to build a 1,600- or 1,700-square-foot wooden house with three small bedrooms and a lockable carport (cars parked on the street have been known to disappear) for only $25,000, though such a budget would dictate that construction take place in a middle-class barrio. Construction in wood can run as low as $16 per square foot. For those with a somewhat larger cookie jar, *International Living* lists a fully furnished home 150 feet from the Caribbean with telephone and satellite TV in a grove of mango, lime, and almond trees for $65,000. When you're ready to look at properties, Eric Pina of Bienes Raices Atlante (tel. 443-1823) or Helen Murphy of Honduras Real Estate (tel. 440-0143) can help you get started.

Because the fruit companies have long influenced the area, good hospitals, fine shops, and community services are firmly established. The quality of medical practice is high, and the Dole-sponsored Hospital Vicente d'Antoni may well be the best in all Central America. Mail service here is better than on the islands, and express mail is prompt and reliable. CURLA, the Regional University Center of the Atlantic Coast, is a center of agricultural study and research and offers an entomology museum displaying over a thousand insect specimens.

The Expats' Bar is your easy-opening wedge into the congenial colony of expatriate residents, perhaps 125 in all. Because the city is next door to the islands, more English is spoken in this bar and this city than anywhere else on the mainland.

La Ceiba may also be called the ecological capital of Honduras. Great national parks and Garifuna villages are near at hand. You can hike in Cuero y Salado National Park, a preserve only 20 miles to the west. There you'll find mangroves, beaches with crocodiles and a protected manatee habitat, and a tropical jungle where you can fraternize with jaguars, pumas, tapirs, toucans, and howler monkeys. Because the park is laced with canals and estuaries, you may wish to rent a canoe.

Similar pleasures are to be enjoyed in the Cataract del Bejuco, falls surrounded by vine-hung forests, as its name implies, and the Pico Bonito National Park, with tapirs and jaguars wandering amidst mahogany and other hardwood trees. To challenge its soaring mountain you'll need a guide and four-wheel drive. Two Garifuna villages, Corozal and Sambo Creek, 8 and 12 miles to the east of the city, are home to some traditional cane-and-thatch houses on stilts as well as restaurants specializing in seafood.

Frank Ford

The owners busy behind the Expats' Bar in La Ceiba

A less energetic but popular pastime is Sunday picnicking on the beach. The best beach is said to be Perú, at a fishing village about six miles east of town. It is adorned with palm trees, grills, and roofed picnic tables for which you pay a nominal fee.

River rafting is popular here. Riding the class II to IV rapids of the Río Sico is exhilarating. Ríos Honduras runs a five-day expedition that includes three nights of camping. If you are living in the city, you should be able to get a reduction in price because you won't need the La Ceiba lodging that is part of the package.

Lions and Kiwanis Clubs give you a chance to network. Afterward you can dance, drink, or gamble the night away. There is a real movie house in the center of town and, just as rare, there's a nine-hole golf course.

La Ceiba is convenient to all parts of Honduras, Mexico, and the United States. As a commercial center with a free zone, it has much to offer the investor-resident as well as the retiree who enjoys urban living. Perhaps more important, La Ceiba is friendlier than most cities.

Trujillo

Trujillo, a town on the North Coast, is even more friendly than La Ceiba. A few hundred yards off the spur road from the main highway are miles and miles of almost untouched beaches lined with palm trees. On both sides approaching town are hotels of markedly different characters, some of them strange, but all good gathering spots for expatriate residents. The landward side of the long entry rises rapidly into breezy foothills. The hilly downtown section is colonial with just a foot in the twentieth century. Pharmacy, bank, Hondutel, and post office stand close together. A block away from the cathedral, a modern hospital lies next to the Fort of Santa Barbara, built in 1599 to repel pirates.

As you press in farther, the town becomes increasingly Caribbean, tin and zinc roofed, a bit shanty and quaint. But you're quickly out the other side, for it's a small town, reposeful and at ease.

Trujillo was the site of the first Mass on the mainland of the Americas, a headquarters for Cortés in 1525, center of the see of the first Honduran bishop, and briefly a shipping channel for gold export. It slumbered fitfully through the next three centuries, occasionally disturbed by attacks by Henry Morgan and other pirates until it attracted world notice in 1860 when William Walker captured it as a toehold toward larger conquests. The bones of that megalomaniac adventurer rest here in the old town cemetery (see the "History of Honduras" chapter).

The town was briefly busy in the banana boom, but that fever ended in the early 1930s when the local banana groves succumbed to Panama disease. For one shining moment during World War II, Trujillo acted as a U.S. naval base.

Today its slender economic base is helped by increased food production in the adjacent valley, but export shipping is mostly handled by a port across the bay. Now the town dreams away, charming the 50 or so expatriates residing in and around it. It will probably never become a resort town. It is too remote. And the town, while always friendly, seems indifferent to tourism, although resort developers, an increasing presence, are said to be beating the bushes.

The seacoast near Trujillo

James D. Gollin

"Paradise" is the description offered by Birkie Campbell, a German-born resident and developer. "Great fun" and "marvelously soothing" are other praises I've heard recently. I didn't interview a single expatriate who was not enthusiastic.

"There's a special warmth here," theorizes Belinda Linton, director of a Trujillo language school. "Part of the appeal is this: Northerners come here from social voids. Many live in little apartments, knowing none of their neighbors, shop in supermarkets or huge, impersonal stores, have few friends with whom they communicate mostly by telephone, and live in and for their work. Here there is a kind of family feeling. People intermingle. At the stores they greet you and say good-bye when you leave. The post office often calls to say you have mail. If you're not well, they stop off with it. Shortly after I first moved here, I discovered that I'd left behind a head of lettuce I'd bought. When I returned to the store, I found the man had it in back, wrapped up in the basket of his bicycle, about to run it up to my house. When I asked if he knew where I lived, he said that everybody did, that here everybody knows everybody."

The kindnesses are self-effacing. I scarcely knew Jorge Brower, who runs the Trujillo Bay Hotel where I stayed briefly. He found me dejectedly kicking the flat tire of the Toyota truck I had rented, disheartened by the knowledge that the spare was under the truck bed. Smiling, he gently prodded me toward the adjoining hotel restaurant, assuring me that troubles seem less after a good breakfast. When I returned after taking his advice, I saw he'd had a strong young man change the tire. By the time I had thankfully pressed an American five-dollar bill on the tire changer—I was later told that that was more than a day's pay to him—Jorge had taken the flat into town and had it repaired. I almost had to force Jorge to accept the ten lempiras (90 cents at that time) the mechanic in town had charged to fix the flat.

That generous spirit seems to be infectious. For example, when Jim Davis, an American resident in Trujillo with whom I'd exchanged no more than a hundred words, heard that my ride to an expatriate's party had fallen through because of the driver's illness, he and his wife drove miles out of their way to pick me up and later return me.

If you're going to stay awhile, especially if you suspect you might decide to live here, a top-notch place to bone up on your Spanish is the Centro Internacional de Idiomas. Up a breezy hillside from town, the center is supervised by owner-director Belinda Linton. Individual instruction takes place in charming little thatched cubicles that look like the jungle huts of the old Tarzan films. For foreigners serious about mastering Spanish, the school supplements class instruction by arranging for students to live with local families. (This opportunity is available in just about every language school in Honduras.) For four hours of classes a day and a week's stay you'll pay only $150.

Linton knows just about everyone in Trujillo and has contacts with several developers. While you're there, introduce yourself to Bill Martin, Belinda's husband. Formerly involved with a cold-stripped steel mill business in New England, he's retired and keeps the school's books. You'll find him an interesting and generous expositor of the quirks and quiddities of Honduras.

The school itself provides further instances of Trujillo kindness. Since it is the only school in Trujillo teaching English, among the students are Spanish-speaking local girls, products of six years of elementary education, who could not afford the tuition. Many receive scholarships from Belinda. Others are sponsored by local stores and the manager of the orphanage. Proficiency in English will later open many doors for these girls at managerial levels in the fruit companies and the hotels.

The approximately 50 expatriate residents of Trujillo are an amiable and well-knit group. The atmosphere is serene and, to my mind, conducive to idleness. The hills above town offer cooling breezes and pleasing possibilities for building a home. Retirees who are sensitive to heat should consider that Trujillo, like La Ceiba, is quite hot in summer. But the town is unquestionably beautiful and likely to remain so. Its remote, end-of-the-road aura makes it an unlikely resort town or obvious tourist target.

To be sure, there are frustrations and lacks. As Bill Martin observes, "You can't get a tire balanced or a key made here." There's little in the way of entertainment. To rent from the town's diminutive supply of videocassettes, you must go to the children's clothing store or the small gym. There's no real department store, just a couple of "supermarkets." There's no car rental, and the local buses are old children's school jalopies from the States. The Laundromat has one washer and one dryer. The one fast-food and take-out shop melted away because the sporadic power caused refrigerator failure. There's no camera shop—surprising because the nationals love cameras and photos—no library, and no bookstore. It will be obvious to any would-be investor that the town has many needs, but whether its small population can support a new enterprise is open to question.

Tela

Also on the coast but to the west of La Ceiba on the way to San Pedro Sula is a charming town that beckons the beach-loving retiree. Once a major banana port, Tela is becoming increasingly interested in its own tourist potential.

The east side, Old Tela (Tela Vieja) looks like a back-lot Hollywood set—a western town of clapboard houses, zinc roofs, and twisting dirt roads. The new or "modern" town to the west of the

James D. Gollin

An inviting Tela beach

river has paved streets and nearby services and becomes suburban as you go west along Ninth Street, the main drag.

Tela's chief attraction is its beachfront, especially on the western side. Miles of powdery sand backed by almost military formations of palm trees seem to be posing for postcard-quality snapshots. You can bathe in either the waters of the lagoon or the ocean salt. As you stand with your back to the water, you are treated to the sight of the lofty peaks of the Nombre de Dios rising about a half mile inland. A national park and botanical gardens are lures to the nature lover. They offer such a variety of sights, sounds, and experiences that it would take years to behold them all.

Because of its former but long connection with United Fruit, the New Tela section of town is somewhat Americanized and has less of a Caribbean flavor. This may or may not attract you as a retiree. But if you seek sunshine and tranquillity, Tela and the sleepy beach towns nearby are ideal. "And you can live in one," promises *International Living*, "for very, very little."

If you're considering investing in this possible boom resort, note that the town is a government-approved tourism project with enormous tax advantages (see the "Investment Possibilities" chapter). On the other hand, you might also note that the roads into and around town could use much improvement, and until they undergo such changes may prove detrimental to any business prospects.

Two Capitals

Almost every tour of Honduras includes the business capital, San Pedro Sula, and the political capital, Tegucigalpa (Tegus). Both cities are large and both set a faster pace than the Bay Islands or the cities of the north coast. Both have modern communications, banking, and medical facilities.

In these cities, in the interior of the mainland, you'll find less English spoken. Even in the government tourist office, few clerks are bilingual. Not only is this Ladino country, but Spanish is the language in common among West Indian, Black Carib, Chinese, Korean, Taiwanese, and Palestinian merchants.

It is the contrasts between the two cities that most strike the visitor. Entering downtown San Pedro by car from a choice of directions (San Pedro, like Rome, is the focus of almost all roads), one is immediately impressed by the neat grid of relatively clean and paved streets controlled by traffic lights on almost every other corner. But venturing from the highway into Tegus, a divider suddenly sends one down a winding, one-way cobblestone street in a torrent of traffic with unmarked intersections angling off every which way.

Since the 30-foot maximum height law applies only to beachfront locations, both cities have tall buildings. San Pedro's business center, constantly rebuilding itself, resembles aggressive North American downtowns, whereas even some of the glassy government buildings of Tegus seem a bit shopworn and shabby—with shacks and shanties just around the corner.

San Pedro is a checkerboard; Tegus is a maze. To the businessman, San Pedro offers more organization and a faster pace, while Tegus seems old-fashioned, inefficient, and caught in tangled political webs.

James D. Gollin

**San Pedro Sula. The town's central plaza
(Parque Central) is seen in the lower left.**

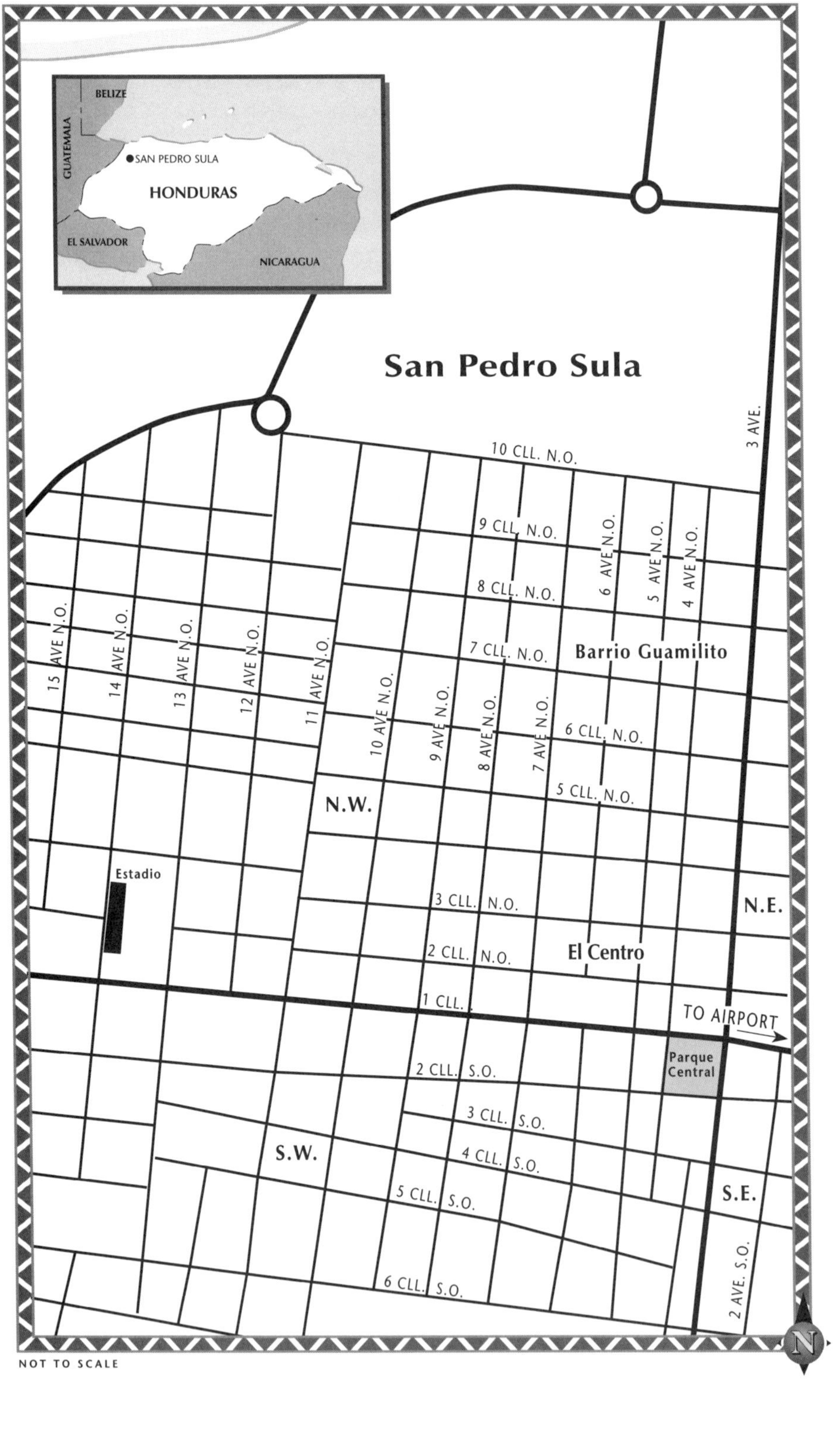

San Pedro Sula

BELIZE
GUATEMALA
●SAN PEDRO SULA
HONDURAS
EL SALVADOR
NICARAGUA

3 AVE.

10 CLL. N.O.
9 CLL. N.O.
8 CLL. N.O.
6 AVE N.O.
5 AVE N.O.
4 AVE N.O.
7 CLL. N.O.   Barrio Guamilito
15 AVE N.O.
14 AVE N.O.
13 AVE N.O.
12 AVE N.O.
11 AVE N.O.
10 AVE N.O.
9 AVE N.O.
8 AVE N.O.
7 AVE N.O.
6 CLL. N.O.
5 CLL. N.O.
N.W.
Estadio
3 CLL. N.O.
N.E.
2 CLL. N.O.   El Centro
1 CLL.
TO AIRPORT
2 CLL. S.O.
Parque
Central
3 CLL. S.O.
S.W.   4 CLL. S.O.
5 CLL. S.O.
S.E.
6 CLL. S.O.
2 AVE. S.O.

N

NOT TO SCALE

On the other hand, San Pedro is flat, low, and hot, while Tegus, at 3,200 feet, is breezy and cooler.

Until recently, Tegucigalpa—although the political capital—was isolated among its mountains, a difficult trek from the coast. The fruit companies never came through with the promised railroad to the interior, and the Pan American Highway follows the easier Pacific coastal route to the south. The banana bonanza, agribusiness, and a railroad hub built in the north over a century ago nurtured the growth of San Pedro but did almost nothing for Tegucigalpa.

San Pedro Sula

San Pedro was founded in 1536 by Pedro de Alvarado, who gave it his saint's name. The "Sula" postscript, tacked on later, may be an Aztec reference to the valley's birds.

San Pedro Sula is Honduras's oldest city and yet the newest. It was ravaged by fire and Indian attacks, savaged by pirates, and almost emptied near the turn of the century by a yellow fever epidemic. Yet there is little of this turbulent past showing in the modern city, the fastest growing in Honduras, which is constantly building and rebuilding. It bustles with the 68,000 new assembly jobs it developed last year. And it flaunts its modernity with its fast-food restaurants, all-night gas stations, and—unfortunately—the highest AIDS rate in Central America (according to the *Wall Street Journal*).

Today San Pedro Sula is the most important distribution point for the northern and western parts of Honduras. Its airport is the busiest and best of the four international airports in the country. Residents can easily access all of Honduras through direct flights on the regional airlines and comfortable trips on modern buses.

A few years ago, San Pedro's population was projected to reach two-thirds of a million by the year 2000, but it has probably already exceeded that mark, so enticing is the city's sweet smell of money. Growing rapidly also is the community of expatriates. You can meet many of them in the remarkably social central plaza (Parque Central).

They bemoan the fact that rental properties are becoming scarce. According to hotel owner Luis Bográn, cheap rentals were common six years ago but now rents are about double those in

Tegucigalpa. I have heard, however, that in the Bel Air neighborhood, a few large, three-bedroom houses have been rented recently for only $800 per month.

Because of the shortage of rentals, managers of new enterprises have to bargain with hotels for monthly rates for non-Honduran employees, so hotel prices for transients and tourists are escalating. All the other costs of living, however, compare favorably with any major city in Latin America.

The banana industry contributed to San Pedro's early growth. More recently, the economic free zone just outside the city has transformed it into a major manufacturing center with generous advantages and exemptions for businesses. Some 20 American-owned companies are turning out export products in this zone at low but somewhat better than average wages. Garments are manufactured here and exported to the United States in great numbers.

You might remember that Kathy Lee Gifford of television talk-show fame caused an uproar a couple of years ago when a congressional hearing disclosed that much of her signature brand clothing sold at Kmart was sewn in Honduran *maquiladoras,* ("sweatshops") by workers receiving some 23 cents an hour! Shortly thereafter, it was discovered that many other garments of her brand were produced by New York sweatshops, which promised workers better wages but failed to pay them at all for weeks. The Honduran workers were certainly poorly paid, but at least they were paid. (To her credit, Gifford and her husband voluntarily ponied up the missing money owed the New Yorkers.)

Though San Pedro Sula is new and businesslike, it lacks architectural interest and colonial charm. Even its cathedral is postwar. Residents (*Sampedranos*), after exploring the city's new archaeological museum, have few other choices. There are several cinemas, a small casino, and a few discotheques. Otherwise, people must recreate mostly outdoors.

Shoppers browse through the handicrafts market. Golfers boast of the city's two golf courses and look forward to the third that is abuilding. For a fee, many hotels provide access to swimming pools and tennis courts. Athletic types can hike in the cloud forest of Parque Nacional Cocuco, 13 miles to the west. But few visitors linger, unless doing business here. Usually they use the city as a jumping-off point for travels elsewhere.

In June, however, the local scene heats up considerably. June Fair is a weeklong party, a tradition here for a century and a half. The city streets fill with parades, Garifuna dancers, drum corps, conch-shell bands, and all kinds of frivolity—exuberantly indulged in by participants in cardboard masks. Food vendors work overtime, and kegs of local beer empty fast. Fiercely contested beauty queen contests promise the winners of various age groups five minutes of celebrity.

Tegucigalpa

Tegucigalpa, or Tegus, more populous then San Pedro Sula with about 850,000 inhabitants, still bears the tailings of its mining days. In 1578 a vein of silver was discovered on Mount Picacho on the north side, and a town sprang up below it almost instantly. Originally called something like "the Royal Site of St. Michael's Mines at Tegucigalpa," the name was mercifully shortened over the years to its present combination of two Nahuatl words: *teguz* (hill) and *galpa* (silver). As recently as 1880, silver accounted for 55 percent of Honduras's exports.

Boomtown growth explains Tegucigalpa's hodgepodge layout, even after local silver mining played out. In 1880 Tegucigalpa took over the role of capital of the country from Comayagua, a town to the northwest halfway down the road to San Pedro. Despite banana company promises, Tegucigalpa has remained a capital without a railroad—indeed, without a highway to the north until 1965.

Tegucigalpa makes a host of different—many of them conflicting—impressions on the first-time visitor and both annoys and entices its residents. It is unquestionably a city, jammed with people, its mountain air tainted with automobile exhaust and the clamor of new construction, its mushrooming *barrios* (neighborhoods) and *colonias* (districts or suburbs) spreading like lava over its many hills, especially toward the airport.

At the same time, it's a colonial Spanish town with a jumble of narrow, winding cobblestone streets prone to potholes, one-way streets innocent of signs or marking, few traffic lights, and vendors selling produce door-to-door. The shaded enclaves of the prosperous are

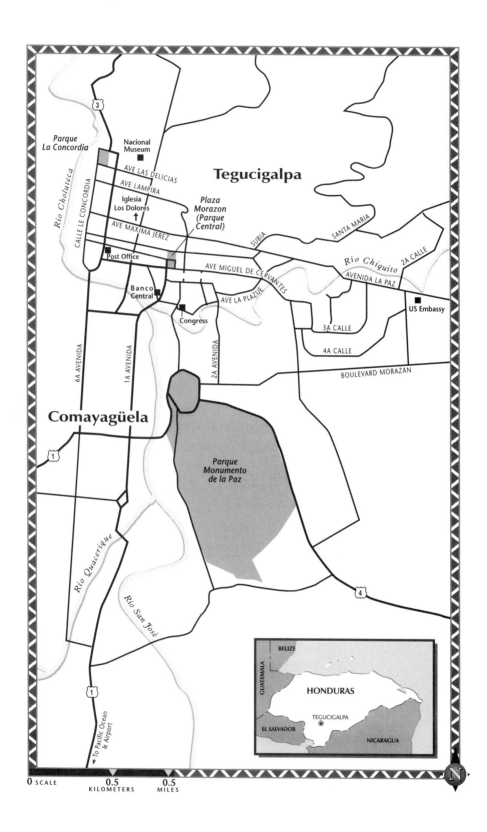

pocketed behind layers of shabby working-class quarters. Despite the flaws in infrastructure, the confusion, and the crowding, property prices in Tegucigalpa are as high as in other Central American capitals.

The congestion and confusion of the inner-city traffic in Tegucigalpa may be considerably relieved by the end of 1998. Carlos Zelaya, minister of public works, transportation, and housing, in 1997 announced a plan to link several barrios directly to the Danlí Highway and to extend the highway itself to Valle de Angeles and its handicraft markets.

Varied fresh-air entertainment is available to the Tegus resident. There are pools, tennis courts, a golf course, and exciting prospects for sightseeing rambles. At Morazán Plaza, numerous species of birds flock in the evening to the delight of bird-watchers. Those who like baseball will be surprised and pleased to find they can watch the great American pastime in Tegucigalpa's new baseball stadium. Those not interested in the baseball can watch the national sport, soccer. (Indeed, every town in Honduras has at least one field consecrated to soccer; Sunday games are fanatically attended by locals.) And almost every town has a billiard hall, for billiards are probably the second favorite Honduran pastime—but a male preference. Female cue wielders are looked at askance.

If cultural activities are vital to your mental and spiritual well-being, Tegus is probably your only choice in Honduras. It has a symphony orchestra, traveling opera, concert halls, art galleries and museums, professional and amateur theaters, and more than a dozen movie houses with first-class films in the original language, most often in English with Spanish subtitles. The city sponsors free films for children. There is even a Toastmasters Club, conducted in English, but with trial speeches allowed in either language. Art groups are active: the women's Mujeres en las Artes conducts cultural excursions in the biosphere of the Tawahka aborinines.Well-stocked American bookstores and English-speaking churches offer clubs and discussion groups.

Add to this the city's charming sectors of colonial architecture, its profusion of small and pleasant parks and malls, a background of towering hills on three sides, and a reputation as one of the safest large cities for travelers in all Central America, and it's enough to cause the tourist to celebrate by noshing at one of the town's many Burger Kings.

Comayaguela is a poorer city across the Río Chaluteca from Tegus. It grew up independently but was joined to Tegus at the turn of the century. (Today the river, destined for the Pacific, is often dry, its water siphoned off for irrigation and its bed providing a place to play ball.) Lively but shabby, with a hubbub of native markets, Comayaguela is a home for the poor and the site of most intercity bus terminals. The markets offer a pleasant daytime diversion, but night jaunts here are considered risky. I know of no American retirees living in this sector.

Lake Yojoa

Another retirement location, rather suburban and country-clubbish, is Lake Yojoa, Honduras's only lake, a beauty spot about 50 miles south of San Pedro. Roughly 14 miles long, 6 miles wide, and 125 feet deep, fed by underground springs, the clear and surprisingly

Beautiful Lake Yojoa

James D. Gollin

warm lake invites swimming, fishing, paddleboating, canoeing, and waterskiing. Lakeside residents have organized sailing clubs and sporting events. You won't find better bass fishing anywhere in the world. Hundreds of different kinds of birds are regulars at the lakeside and seem to pose deliberately for bird-watchers.

Residents can manage without cars. The fast buses on the San Pedro–Tegucigalpa run pick them up or drop them off at the restaurant at the northeast corner of the lake. Frequent smaller buses serve passengers along the northeastern side and continue on a mile or two to the town of Peña Blanca, where residents go for gas, banks, and a pharmacy.

A secondary road to the north of Peña Blanca leads to postcard-like Pulhapanzak Falls, 135 feet of spectacular cascades, with swimming and picnicking spots in a lush tropical setting, all part of Santa Barbara National Park with its cloud forest and the formidable Mount Marancho. Sugarcane, pineapple, and coffee plantations circle the area, possible opportunities for the investment-minded.

The lake area has charm and the advantage of proximity to a large city. At an elevation of 1,900 feet, its weather is generally benign. It rains heavily in October and November, but usually at night. For lake-lovers this might be an ideal locale for settling down. Who knows, it might some day rival Lake Chapala in Mexico as an expatriate haven!

Three More Favorites

The three towns I'm going to describe next are favorites for their special beauty, charming atmosphere, and *simpático* way of life. But I must warn you that if you decide to live in any of them, or even to make a visit of more than a few hours, you will be "going native."

You will need a fair fluency in Spanish and considerable self-reliance. Few residents know any English, the population of expatriates is small, and it's the rare restaurant that serves food similar to American cuisine. The *hospedades* (hotels) are often clean but usually bare, poorly lit, and lacking amenities, occasionally even hot water. They seldom accept credit cards.

On the other hand, a room with a bath in the best hotel in

town can be rented for very little, usually less than $200 per month. If you prefer your own house, the cost of land and construction is much cheaper than in the cities. The townspeople offer friendly welcomes, and it's possible to form close relationships with the local Ladino society.

Two of my favorites, Siguatepeque and La Esperanza, are found off the highway between San Pedro Sula and Tegucigalpa. If you are heading south to Tegus, look for signs at about the halfway point—about an hour and half's drive. Siguatepeque is just a long stone's throw east of the highway. La Esperanza is another 40 miles west, along a winding and hilly dirt and gravel road; easier access is via the road south from Santa Rosa de Copán, the third favorite town.

La Esperanza

La Esperanza is set on a partially forested plateau. The town's low adobe houses, barracks by the central plaza, striking church clock tower, dirt roads, and quiet quaintness will take you back in time. Because it is the administrative center of the state of Intibucá, a name shared with the Amerindian district of the town, it provides banking and municipal services.

Sunday is the liveliest day in La Esperanza, when the colorful traditional market overflows the town. Locals turn out in full force, and their ranks are doubled by Lenca Indians toting their wares from miles around. There are public swimming areas nearby, just outside La Gruta. At La Posona you can rent a boat and fish.

The town's lofty perch ensures a springlike climate year-round. But most people—other than anthropologists devoted to studying the Lenca Indians—will find this backwater town a bit too laid-back for anything but a hammock retirement.

Siguatepeque

Siguatepeque, at 3,700 feet, has some noticeably hot (but not torrid) days with an average daytime high of 81°F. Nights are about twenty degrees cooler, so neither fans nor heating is needed. The air is untainted and invigorating.

With a population of about 35,000, the city offers friendliness and a lively community feeling. Since it is halfway between San Pedro Sula and Tegucigalpa, the resident can reach either city in about an hour and a half.

Coming in from the highway, you will pass a colorful cemetery. I mean that "colorful" literally—with bright crypts and vaults worth a photographic study. Then you will come to a large and lovely central park, with shade trees, a modern church, and a native market. Keep going on the main street and you will encounter some twenty blocks crammed with shops and supermarkets, banks and pharmacies, a large clinic and a homeopathic medical center, a radio station advertised as "more powerful," public and private bilingual schools, a laundry, a government home for the retired, a gas station, a lumberyard, a few restaurants, many *comedores*, and several hotels.

The Evangelical Hospital is modern and highly regarded. A visit to a doctor in a private clinic here costs between $2 and $10. A taxi to your doctor from anywhere in town will cost less than 50 cents. According to Richard Miller, a five-year resident, banking and postal service are reliable. In the excellent bilingual school (through the secondary level), about half the staff are North American or British. Miller assures the retiree that one can rent, buy, or build here for about a third of the cost in the States.

Santa Rosa de Copán

Leaving Copán heading east, there's a fork in the road at La Entrada. Taking the fork south for 20 miles of recently paved road will put you in Santa Rosa de Copán, a pleasant colonial town enjoying the cool mountain air at 3,500 feet. So calmly dignified is this town, that no one would suspect that it's the political center of western Honduras.

The cobbled streets, red-tile roofs, and beautiful setting may tempt you to linger and, if you're a smoker, enjoy one of the local hand-rolled cigars. Nearby is the long-ago seat of the colonial government of all Central America, Gracias, where you might go for an ice-cream sundae at the Guancascos Restaurant. In the neighborhood are artesian springs, a small lake and ponds, a forest preserve, and caves. The town's Hotel Elvir arranges trips in the area. I have heard that some expatriates have settled here, but I have yet to meet any.

10

▼▲▼▲▼▲▼▲▼▲▼▲▼▲▼▲▼▲▼▲▼▲▼▲▼▲▼▲▼▲▼▲▼▲▼

Laws of Residency, Investment, and Land Ownership

The "banana republic" of Honduras has become one of the last places on earth where a foreigner can own an affordable piece of paradise. Here more than anywhere, foreign investors enjoy a plethora of advantages and freedoms in starting their businesses.

Suspicion of foreigners had been the tenor of the official outlook for most of the last generation. That's understandable when you consider that immigration had been a thorn in the side of Honduras since the mid-1960s—when an influx of over 300,000 undocumented Salvadorians caused great public unrest, heated labor disputes, and, in part, the Soccer War of 1969.

The following decade saw the incredibly vicious and bloody civil war in El Salvador between the military—brutal and extremely rightist, growing alarmingly with U.S. aid—and the fiercely Marxist

FMLN backed by Cuba and the Soviet Union. Rightist death squad carnage, including the assassination of priests, nuns, and a beloved bishop, aroused world concern with little internal effect. At the start of this decade, a cease-fire and an accord have forced the two groups to try to settle their differences in the political arena rather than on the battlefields.

Honduras's worries were compounded during the 1980s by other intruders: Nicaraguans fleeing a horrifying revolution in their land, some 15,000 Contras fighting the Sandanistas, and pro-Cuban and pro-Soviet Marxists. Not until free elections in Nicaragua in 1990 resulted in the defeat of Daniel Ortega and the Sandanistas did tensions ease. The changed circumstances enabled the disbanding of the burdensome Contras.

At last, Hondurans and their new president, Rafael Callejas, could draw an easier breath and focus their attention on an economy unimproved by years of profligate military aid. Officials began to welcome tourism and foreign residency and devised ways of actively encouraging enterprise and foreign investment—uninfluenced by political and international puppet strings.

Along with the newly enterprising attitude has come legislation—laws pertinent to residency, investment, and land ownership. This chapter will attempt to review and clarify these laws.

Pensionates and Rentists

On August 6, 1991, the Honduran Congress passed Decree 93-91, entitled "Law for the Pensionates and Rentists." It superseded previous decrees that were more restrictive and that stated financial requirements in Honduran lempiras, since devalued. The decree warns all residents, however, that the privilege of residency could be canceled for non-compliance with the law, use of false documents in the application, or activities that threaten national security or public order.

One type of residency long precedes this decree, a right recognized by almost every country in the world—that of residency by virtue of marriage to a native. It is not, however, automatic. An application is required with the marriage. A second type of residency through acquired citizenship is open to all who are Central Americans by birth. After a year of residence in Honduras they are considered citizens by naturalization.

Decree 93-91 covers all immigrants who wish to establish some sort of residency status in Honduras. "Pensionates" (*pensionados*) are retirees who wish to be accepted as legal residents of Honduras. The provisions are almost identical to the *pensionado* program, now repealed, that once made Costa Rica a magnet for foreign retirees. The pensionates must prove that they are truly retired, that they will not seek or take employment in Honduras, and that they have a permanent and stable income derived from abroad or from the Honduran national banking system of no less than $600 per month. Obviously, this money can come from Social Security or a company pension.

The "rentist resident" (*rentista*)—a person of independent means whose income comes from such sources as stocks, bonds, real estate, or inheritance—must prove a sure monthly income (presumably by some annuity arrangement guaranteed for a minimum of ten years) of at least $1,000.

The law, without raising the ante, allows successful applicants to bring an entire family—spouse, dependents, single children under

Bill Martin at a Trujillo home

18, and handicapped children or students under 25—into Honduras under the same monetary umbrella.

The general retirement provisions apply not only to foreigners but also to native Hondurans who have worked for international organizations or foreign governments and have resided abroad "permanently" (at least ten years). So long as they can prove that they have retired with a secure and sufficient pension or have accumulated enough funds to provide a rentist's annuity, they receive the same benefits.

Requirements of Residency

Once your residency visa is granted, that proven secure income is put to practice. These minimum amounts—$600 or $1,000—must be deposited monthly at the Honduran Central Bank or any other national institution. Furthermore, they must be converted into lempiras.

Both pensionates and rentists must reside in Honduras for at least four consecutive months each year. If, because of extraordinary problems, residents can't comply with this requirement, they must ask the Department of Tourism for a waiver and convert enough funds to the local currency to satisfy the monthly conversion requirement during their absence. Those who have fulfilled the four-month residency stipulation must do the same whenever they leave the country.

Without certification by the Department of Tourism, immigration officials will not permit departure from the country. Those who skip the monthly conversion rule for more than two months will find their names published as delinquent in *La Tribuna*. Prolonged failure to comply may cause cancellation of residency. The four-month stay and the required deposit of the mandated amount of funds during absence are musts for all immigrant residents, except "Daddy Warbucks" investors described below.

Benefits of Residency

Jubilado is the charming title given to a retiree who has passed his 65th birthday. (The English cognates *jubilee* and *jubilation* are certainly more pleasant associations than "senior citizen.") In a recent piece of legislation called the Third Age (*Tercera Edad*)—another pleasant euphemism—the Honduran congress has provided a host of benefits for such residents.

The jubilant retiree is issued a special card that entitles him to a variety of discounts on public utilities, medicines and drugs, cinemas and theater, legal fees, and travel from Honduras to the nearest "port of call," which on the airlines means Miami, Houston, or New Orleans. This is a generous gesture, but affordable since presently only 4 percent of nationals pass that golden birthday.

Legislative interest in senior citizenship is new to Honduras, so whether these privileges apply to non-Honduran citizens is a matter of some dispute. There are reports of a number of North Americans who have been able to avail themselves of them, and the present

RESIDENCY BASICS

Benefits of Residency

- Dispensa (right to import household goods and automobile exempt from customs duties and import taxes)
- Foreign income exempt from Honduran income tax
- Residency card facilitating entry, exit, and prolonged stay
- Passport privileges after three years

Residency Requirements

- $600 or $1,000 must be deposited monthly and converted into lempiras
- Proof of retirement
- Affirmation that individual will not seek or take employment in Honduras
- Proof of secure and sufficient pension or other annual income
- Residence in Honduras for at least four consecutive months each year, investing required monthly amount

▼▲▼

legislative plans seem disposed to clarify and extend the necessary authorization.

Aside from the Third Age provisions, pensionates and rentists, both foreign and native, receive other benefits. (By the way, the categories of pensionate and rentist can be interchanged either way as time or circumstances dictate.) First, the foreign income declared by pensionates and rentists is exempt from Honduran income tax. Second, these persons and their dependents have the right, one time only, to bring in all their household furnishings exempt from customs duties and import taxes (which can run as high as 40 percent of value).

Included in this exemption (called the *dispensa*) is a car imported for personal use. And, in theory, the old lemon may be replaced with a new import every five years with the same beneficial exemptions. (Such is the freedom under the law, but several residents report it "more honored in the breach than in the observance.")

Third, transplants are issued a card from the Immigration Department that identifies them as residents and dispenses with the need for tourist stamps or short-lived visas. This card is renewed every two years by the Institute of Tourism.

After you have resided in Honduras for three consecutive years, you may apply for a Honduran passport. This allows you the same freedom of entrance and egress that a Honduran citizen enjoys, except that monthly deposits are still expected. The passport does not make you a citizen, nor does it permit you to vote, but neither does it threaten your American citizenship.

A passport does, however, allow you to apply for honorary Honduran citizenship. Even this privilege, granted for special services or because of marriage to a Honduran, will not invalidate your American citizenship. You are not swearing a new allegiance but simply pledging to comply with Honduran law. For some years now the United States has been permitting its citizens to hold a second passport along with a courtesy citizenship without prejudice or penalty. A possible fly in the ointment is a provision in the present Honduran constitution that forbids dual citizenships. Although almost never mentioned, it could be invoked against you. Make sure your "citizenship" is honorary, not full.

There are a few more catches. First, to avoid profiteering by the *dispensa*, new residents may not sell the furnishings or cars they bring in for three years. Otherwise, the waiver will be annulled and sellers will have to pay full duties on those goods retroactively. However, if robbery, accident, collision, or fire causes loss of a vehicle within five

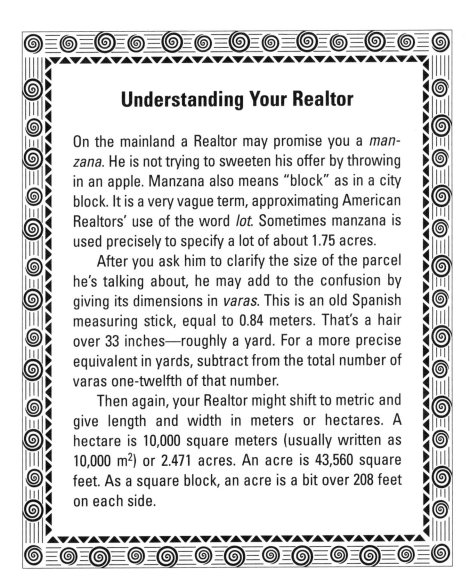

Understanding Your Realtor

On the mainland a Realtor may promise you a *manzana*. He is not trying to sweeten his offer by throwing in an apple. Manzana also means "block" as in a city block. It is a very vague term, approximating American Realtors' use of the word *lot*. Sometimes manzana is used precisely to specify a lot of about 1.75 acres.

After you ask him to clarify the size of the parcel he's talking about, he may add to the confusion by giving its dimensions in *varas*. This is an old Spanish measuring stick, equal to 0.84 meters. That's a hair over 33 inches—roughly a yard. For a more precise equivalent in yards, subtract from the total number of varas one-twelfth of that number.

Then again, your Realtor might shift to metric and give length and width in meters or hectares. A hectare is 10,000 square meters (usually written as 10,000 m^2) or 2.471 acres. An acre is 43,560 square feet. As a square block, an acre is a bit over 208 feet on each side.

years, the resident may purchase another vehicle under the same tax-exempt umbrella.

Furthermore, because Honduras does not want foreigners competing with its nationals in the job market, the law does not permit immigrant residents to work for pay. In practice, however, many immigrants earn money by forming incorporated businesses and becoming investor residents (see below). Corporations investing in tourism, housing, industry, or agriculture are very welcome.

One type of pensionate resident is free to work without restriction. Persons who offer their professional services to "government entities, autonomous or semi-autonomous agencies, universities, or technical or superior education centers" may work and receive pay. Such people are thought to be performing services for which they are uniquely qualified and so are not competing with Honduran workers. Their Honduran pay, however, is subject to Honduran income tax.

Investor Residents

Like the older laws on residency, legislation governing foreign investment in Honduras used to be very restrictive. Take the example of Jim Davis of Trujillo: As his nursery business expanded and he became the largest exporter of Spanish moss to the States, government red tape and pressure increased to such an extreme that he closed his Honduran operation and shifted all his activities to his partnership holdings in Nicaragua.

But with peace among Honduras's neighbors and stability in the domestic political scene, recent years have seen extraordinary changes in the investment laws. Decree 93-91 created the category of "investor resident," one who has complied with the rentist requirement and, working within Honduran corporation law, invests in productive activities such as industry, agriculture, housing, or tourism. As evidence of good faith, the applicant for investor residency deposits $1,000 in a Honduran bank.

Normally, the immigrant investor may not work behind a counter or on the floor, unless he can show that he is uniquely qualified for that position with no available Honduran substitute or that he is training nationals in their duties and responsibilities. The investor resident does not receive the privileges of the *dispensa* and usually pays Honduran income tax on local income. (An exception is made for those who invest in tourism.)

At the municipality office, the investor will be asked his income and will be told the corresponding tax. The following year, the office will expect about the same income. (I have twice heard the scandalous rumor of Americans stating their income in accurate figures—say, "40,000"—but allowing the tax office to think that they were speaking of lempiras.)

Recently the government is allowing 100 percent foreign ownership of corporations, including limited partnerships. The services of a bilingual Honduran lawyer are vital to the investor resident. Finding a reliable one is best done by networking.

The "Daddy Warbucks" Resident

An investor who pledges one million lempiras (almost $76,000) to spend on land, buildings, vehicles, or equipment in a new business falls into a category I call the "Daddy Warbucks" resident. As his plans go forward and undergo official scrutiny, a good-faith deposit of almost half the total amount is to be entrusted to a Honduran bank.

Detailed plans and a work schedule must be submitted to the Immigration Office and the Ministry of Economy and Commerce. Approval of the proposed activity is likely, so long as it is considered productive and is on a fairly large scale. An influx of mom-and-pop stores (*pulperias*) is not the intention. In fact, a 1992 decree states, "Small-scale industry and commerce is exclusive patrimony of Hondurans and of partnerships totally made up of Hondurans." One type of industry is specifically forbidden: the production of firearms or weapons of any kind.

Major investors can bring in family and dependents like all other residents. Additionally, they may bring in technicians or other specialists necessary for the operation of the business, as long as these specialists do not comprise more than 10 percent of the workforce.

▼▲▼▲▼▲▼▲▼▲▼▲▼▲▼▲▼▲▼▲▼▲▼▲▼▲▼▲▼▲▼▲▼▲▼▲▼

(Ninety percent of the total employee roster must be Honduran, and their pay must equal 85 percent of the total payroll.)

This investor is released from the monthly conversions required of the others, provided that the entire principal amount of the pledge has been converted by the rentist or a duly authorized representative within one year. After the person is registered as an investor with the Ministries of the Economy and Immigration, he or she receives a card verifying the new status. This card, renewable annually, allows unrestricted passage to and from the country.

Should you be considering any of the investor-rentist categories, you can now do one-stop shopping for approval and permission of your project. Decree 80-92 has set up a single office in the Ministry of Economy and Commerce to assist the investor in all matters related to his investment. All other government agencies are instructed to cooperate with this ministry with regard to investment requirements.

If you see yourself as an investor, you may be heartened to know that the IRS exempts from U.S. income tax the first $70,000 of yearly income earned abroad by a citizen or a U.S. resident alien who is a bona fide resident of that foreign country for a full tax year or who is physically present in foreign countries for at least 330 full days during any consecutive 12 months. You may also deduct certain

▼▲▼▲▼▲▼▲▼▲▼▲▼▲▼▲▼▲▼▲▼▲▼▲▼▲▼▲▼▲▼▲▼▲▼▲▼

FREE ZONE BENEFITS

- Companies that are 100 percent export may import all needed materials and equipment without duties. They are exempt from income, city, county, sales, and corporate taxes.
- Companies working within Private Export Processing Zones pay no taxes and no customs duties on imported materials or exported products.
- Tourism-related businesses don't pay income taxes for 20 years and are exempt from the local 7 percent sales tax on building materials. Imported materials for the project are duty free.

▲▼▲▼▲▼▲▼▲▼▲▼▲▼▲▼▲▼▲▼▲▼▲▼▲▼▲▼▲▼▲▼▲▼▲▼▲

foreign housing costs. Furthermore, any Honduran taxes you must pay are deductible from your U.S. liability.

New Incentives and Free Zones

The privileges of investor residents have been additionally detailed and clarified by Decree 80-92. Its preamble offers a policy of increased inducements and reduced government intervention to "promote production, transfer technology, increase exports and create employment to benefit the Honduran population."

The decree promises equal and nondiscriminatory treatment of all private enterprise, whether capitalized by Hondurans, foreigners, or coinvestors, and provides an adequate legal and administrative framework to guarantee security in investments. Foreign investors have the historical reassurance that foreign enterprises have never been nationalized by Honduras.

The revised Free Zone Law, originally established in 1976, now offers remarkable freedoms. Puerto Cortés, Omoa, Choloma, Tela, La Ceiba, and Amapala are all free zones. So long as companies operating there are 100 percent export, they may import all needed material, equipment, office supplies, and the like without any duties, and they are exempt from income, city, county, sales, and corporate taxes. (Individual salaries are not exempt.) The companies may repatriate their money without restriction and may conduct their business with minimal paperwork. Usable local raw materials, such as wood, leather, and spices, are available at very low cost. Companies may construct their own buildings there, provided they are fenced and secure. An annual fee for the permit is paid to the Honduran Port Authority. Buildings rent for as little as $2 per square foot. Convenient municipal services already exist. The advantage to Honduras in this boon, of course, is jobs for its hordes of unemployed.

A recent extension of the law allows for the establishment of Private Export Processing Zones anywhere in the country. Companies complying with these laws can set up in private zones outside the already established free zones. There are at least 10 private industrial parks within an hour of San Pedro Sula. Rentals there run

$3–$5 per square foot, depending on services. Within these zones, companies pay no taxes and no customs duties on imported materials or exported products, and face no restrictions on the use of foreign exchange or repatriation of capital or profits. In 1992 companies operating outside the zones but devoted entirely to export were granted similar privileges of free import and export and exemption from national income tax for up to 10 years. However, city taxes and a customs broker fee must be paid.

In 1993 the Intellectual Property Rights Law promised protection of foreign copyrights, trademarks, and patents. Furthermore, the formation of public and private corporations and limited partnerships, even though totally foreign, was made lawful, so long as the workforce is 90 percent Honduran, earning 85 percent of the total payroll.

Tourism Projects Blessed

The government has come to realize how much revenue tourism can bring in. So, for such ventures as hotels, apartment houses, and bed-and-breakfasts, the Tourist Free Zone Law offers the same financial benefits as the Private Export Processing Zones law.

Should you propose a tourism-related investment, your proposal will be studied carefully for environmental impact. If your proposal is accepted, you'll pay no income tax on your profits for 20 years, and you'll be exempt from the local 7 percent sales tax on your building materials. Furthermore, you may import all the materials and equipment needed for your project duty-free—including some items that would otherwise incur a tariff as high as 120 percent of cost! You will pay a 1 percent asset tax on the capital registered after two years of business. Since this law also permits the importation of motor vehicles, boats, and airplanes for use within the zone, it opens a way for the investor-resident to bring in his automobile duty-free, so long as it will be used in the tourist trade.

As always, patience is needed. Before pursuing any tourist business, you must form a corporation and assemble the following documents: corporation papers, power of attorney, copy of the land survey, title to that land, and a set of plans for development. The approval process can take as long as a year and cost as much as 10 percent of your total investment. *International Living* suggests getting in contact with the director general for foreign trade, Herman Reichle (tel. 239-2123), who wields a sharp scissors for red tape.

Whether you have taken your first trip or not, if you even suspect you might be interested in investment with or without a residency, write or call the Foundation for Investments and Development of Exports (FIDE), also known as the Industrial Development Group-Honduras. It's a nonprofit organization dedicated to nurturing the development of Honduras and is a good source of information about business opportunities and contacts. FIDE will arrange itineraries for you and set up meetings. (See sidebar on page 167)

Purchase of Land for Housing

There are a number of restrictions on foreign ownership of land, but you need not be a resident. Most important are your satisfaction with the area and your acceptance of the property as it is (promises of improvement tend to vaporize after signing). Caution: Don't sign any document written only in English; it won't hold up in court. A bilingual lawyer is a necessity.

A nonnative Honduran may not, as an individual, own more than one property in his name unless he has acquired others by inheritance. He may acquire property on land designated as "urban" that does not exceed 3,000 square meters in area (a bit less than three-quarters of an acre or 32,265 square feet), or he may buy up to 3,000 square meters of "waste" land that the local municipality has determined to be national.

If a non-Honduran buys property on waste land to build a house, he is enjoying the result of 1991 legislation that empowered municipalities to sell national land within municipal boundaries so long as there was no private ownership. The proposed house must be completed within 36 months of purchase of the land, unless delayed by an "act of God," or the owner will be subjected to an annual surtax of 20 percent of the appraised value of the property until completion. If he purchases urban land to build a house for occasional or permanent housing, he has the same obligation to complete building within 36 months.

Tracts of Land

If the non-Honduran wants a bigger piece of land or more than one tract, whether for personal or investment reasons, he must form a corporation—limited partnership or stock—to own it. A stock corporation is less complex than a limited partnership, and is generally recommended. Ownership is represented by stock certificates.

Corporations not entirely formed by Hondurans must observe all restrictions, modalities, and prohibitions established for these corporate instruments by the secretary of state. The purchaser of urban land, whether a person or a corporation, must submit documents fully identifying him or the company to the Institute of Tourism. The corporation must fully document the identities of all shareholders and their extent of financial interest and control. It must submit a property deed, promissory note of sale or pre-contract, record of the official land register from the relevant municipality, and a complete description of the planned project including technical and feasibility studies.

An authorized notary must furnish reliable proof of the nationality of all shareholders of a company, and that proof must be accepted by a Honduran registry office with its registration copied onto the title or deed. In the case of an individual buyer, he must include proof of his nationality. If urban land is purchased, the foreign company need not present that statement.

The appropriate Land Register office must notify the Institute of Tourism of a new registration within 30 days and must forward a copy of the property deed or title. The company selling the property must notify the institute of any stock owned by a non-Honduran and of any non-Honduran memberships in the purchaser corporation. Any non-Honduran purchaser has the same obligation to inform the institute within 60 days.

Buyers must submit project plans for approval within 12 months of land purchase or face a fine of 20 percent of the appraised value of the property. Approval will only be granted if the use of such property and construction is of benefit to tourism, economic or social development, or the public interest.

Whether a private dwelling or a condominium, the finished work must be ecologically sound and must be in accord with the regulations of the municipality in which it is located. Sale of the land or house must be authorized, and the new owner must pledge completion and compliance with all the obligations imposed on the previous owner.

At this point I'll quote a premonition recently voiced by *International Living*: "Locals are beginning to be more wary of foreigners buying up vast tracts of the country, and if it becomes a really hot political issue, then law makers are likely to close up the loopholes the decree presently ignores. It's an issue worth following."

Buyer Beware

What all this means is that you'll need a skilled, trustworthy, bilingual lawyer to help you purchase land in Honduras. Be sure to network extensively, especially with expatriates, before you settle on one. The same advice applies to choosing a Realtor.

In dealing with lawyers and Realtors, don't hesitate to ask for references and names of people with whom they have recently done business. Don't let yourself be rushed, and be especially careful of claims that an offer is unique and the last one of its type in all Honduras. Remember that you are a stranger in a strange land.

You must also be extremely careful about the search for the title and deed. Title disputes are frequent in Honduras, especially in the Bay Islands—Guanaja above all. A prospective buyer must secure an accurate survey and conduct a painstaking title search.

11

▼▲▼▲▼▲▼▲▼▲▼▲▼▲▼▲▼▲▼▲▼▲▼▲▼▲▼▲▼▲▼▲▼▲▼▲▼

Making the Move

Residency in Honduras is not necessary if you wish to buy land, build or purchase a house, or invest. You can do all of these things on a succession of visas. On the other hand, if you do become a resident, you are free from monthly stamping of your visa or travel permit and the necessity of leaving the country for three days every six months so as to reenter on a new visa.

If you do become a resident you'll be required to deposit the equivalent of $600 per month, $1,000 per month if you are a rentist. Even if you leave the country for months on end, you must deposit sufficient funds for the time you're absent. The law threatens loss of resident status for repeated noncompliance. No one, so far as I know, has suffered this ultimate sanction.

The benefits of residency are both psychological—you are officially recognized as belonging in Honduras—and material. With your resident card you can pass through customs more easily and without having to get a travel-permit stamp in your passport. Your status as a resident also makes you seem like a more reliable business partner.

The chief benefit to the *pensionado* or *rentista* resident—not the investor—is the *dispensa*, the right to import all household goods and furnishings, as well as a vehicle, free of duty. This translates into enormous savings. Furthermore, three years of such residency enables you to obtain a Honduran passport and citizenship. Your residency card can also speed the lengthy process of obtaining permission to bring in the family pet or firearms.

Applying for Residency

The process of applying for residency can be long, cumbersome, and, in some cases, fairly expensive, but it can be eased by following the advice of those who have already been through the mill. Therefore, if during your first trip to Honduras you think it's possible that you may apply, quiz every immigrant resident you meet for shortcuts and clarifications and for the names of reliable Honduran attorneys.

Start the process six months before you intend to move. Even then you will have to call on all your reserves of patience. The speed with which your application will be processed is unpredictable; it's not uncommon for a couple applying together to receive individual approval several months apart. It is often joked that Honduran consulates in North America need operator's manuals. Lists of requirements differ from consulate to consulate, and some are more specific than others.

Consulates are bureaucracies, and rigidity and negative mind-sets are not uncommon amongst those who run them. Also, translated applications can be difficult to understand. The English instructions sent by the consulates are often nebulous; the English terms used, less than exact. As with subtitled English or Spanish films, the translation often misses some of the precision and connotations of the original.

You may run into other problems as well. Bob and Karen Schrey, Canadians by birth but longtime United States citizens, were doubly burdened in their application process. Bob, born in Calgary of American parents, had to get his birth certificate from the American consulate in Calgary then have it notarized by an American attorney and sent to the Canadian Department of External Affairs to be certified as a valid document. Only then could he send it to the Honduran embassy for authentication. "I went through this with about 10 documents for each of us," Bob recalls. "And the Honduran embassy charged $50 for each document they authenticated. On the whole, it was a long and rather expensive business. Now I know enough to save three months' time." Almost all expatriate residents profess knowledge of time-saving tips, so it's important to network with them on your first visit.

You should be understanding and courteous with your Honduran lawyer. To an American, 30 days means 30 days. Not so to a Honduran. Anxious to please you, he may unwittingly impede the

HONDURAN CONSULATES IN THE UNITED STATES

Washington, D.C.
(embassy and consulant)
3007 Tibtilden Street NW
Washington, D.C. 20008
(202) 966-7702

New York
80 Wall Street, Suite 415
New York, NY 10005
(212) 269-3611

Coral Gables
300 Sevilla Avenue, Suite 201
Coral Gables, FL 33134
(305) 447-6375

New Orleans
World Trade Center
2 Canal Street, Suite 1641
New Orleans, LA 70130
(504) 522-3118

Houston
4151 Southwest Freeway,
Suite 700
Houston, TX 77027
(713) 622-4572

Chicago
2000 N. Racine, Suite 2110
Chicago, IL 60614
(773) 472-8726

San Francisco
870 Market Street, Suite 449
San Francisco, CA 94102
(415) 392-0076

Los Angeles
3450 Wilshire Boulevard,
Suite 230
Los Angeles, CA 90010
(213) 383-9244

progress of your application. Attempting to browbeat him is counter-productive. If your lawyer dislikes you, he can bring the process to a near standstill. Don't begin shipping your household goods before the application process is finished. Furniture can pile up on the dock long before your residency permit comes through.

Although it is now possible to start the application process at the Honduran Institute of Tourism in Tegucigalpa, the customary way to begin is with the Honduran consulate nearest you. In the United States consulates are located in Washington, D.C., New York, Coral Gables, New Orleans, Houston, Chicago, San Francisco, and Los Angeles. In Canada consulates can be found in both Montreal and Ottawa. In other countries of Central America, South America, and Europe, if Honduran consulates are present, they can be found in the capital city. The exception is Spain, where there are consulates in both Madrid and Barcelona. There are also consulates in Taipei, Seoul, Cairo, and Tel Aviv.

Necessary Documents

First, a *Solicitud de Ingreso como Inmigrante* (Application for Entry as an Immigrant), available from the consulate for $150 per person, must be filled out and presented with official stamps affixed. Besides such expected questions as name, address, telephone, birth date, nationality, marital status, occupation, and names and ages of minor children, there are short-essay questions asking the purpose of your trip, your reasons for wishing to reside in Honduras, and whether you have any close relatives in Honduras.

Confusingly, a question about your financial resources is tied in with the implication that you will be an investor. If you are applying as a retiree, presumably the answer is that you are not asking for investor status. Of course, if you are applying as an investor or have a contract for a job and need a work permit, your answers will differ from the retiree's. Or, as a retiree, you may be interested in investing in tourism, housing, or agricultural activities. If so, you should indicate your intentions at this point.

The second document is your birth certificate, notarized and

Applying for the Dispensa

To apply for the dispensa—tax exemption for importing your personal household goods and automobile into Honduras—you must submit the following:

1. Photocopy of the residency certificate or resolution issued by the Honduran Institute of Tourism.
2. Eight copies of the list of household goods on a form provided by the institute. The list may be in English. The institute will translate the list for customs, but it might be wise to have a bilingual lawyer double check the translation. All lists must be signed. Port and country of origin must be specified as well as port or customs office in Honduras at which your possessions will arrive.
3. Eight copies describing your automobile, plus a certified copy proving ownership (the title). The same requirements for signature and information as to origin and destination apply here as in #2.
4. A fiscal stamp of 10 lempiras.

The dispensa doesn't cover shipping. If you take your car to Tampa, Florida, then send it to Honduras from there, expect to pay about $600 to get it to Puerto Cortés and about $700 to get it to Roatán.

If some of the above details seem a bit hazy, blame it on trying to reconcile instructions I received from two different consulates. The directions from your consulate may be different still. Follow them, and good luck!

affixed with the county clerk's stamp. If you are applying as a family, the birth records of spouse and dependents under age 18 must be included. Copies, varying in number, will be requested by the consulate.

Third, you must supply a valid passport, four passport-size photographs, and photographs of everyone included in your application. You'll also need a document certifying civil status (married, single, divorced, etc.) of each applicant. For students, who must be under 25, you'll need certificates of student status.

Fourth, if your spouse is included in the application, you must supply your original marriage certificate as well as three copies. If your spouse intends to apply as an investor, he or she must file separately.

Fifth, you must supply a notarized report (and three copies) of "good conduct" showing that you have no criminal record for the last six months.

Sixth, you must provide notarized statements (and three copies) demonstrating a regular pension or Social Security income of at least $600 per month. If you apply as a rentist you must also supply a notarized statement from a bank, insurance company, or annuity fund assuring a secure $1,000 per month from investments in non-Honduran sources. The original decree says the income must be assured for at least ten years. But consular statements say "on a permanent basis," presumably for life.

APPLYING FOR RESIDENCY: NECESSARY DOCUMENTS

- *Solicitud de Ingresso como Inmigrante* (Application for Entry as an Immigrant)
- birth certificate
- passport and photographs
- marriage certificate
- report of good conduct (no criminal record)
- proof of regular pension or Social Security income
- certificate of good health

Add to these a notarized certificate (and copies) of good health. If you have a disability, this is where it should be specified. You will also have to provide copies of your contract, if you are moving to Honduras for a job. Some consulates may even ask for copies of your income tax return.

Last are two documents for which you must appear in person at the consulate. On one you testify that you are not a Communist. On the other you pledge to abide by Honduran law while in the country.

Buying Your Corner of Heaven

Because you are not just moving but transplanting, you should get a good feel for the place, the culture, and the community before you purchase any land in Honduras. Although some people have been content with purchases made on their first exploratory visit, prudence dictates more experience is necessary than any tour is likely to provide.

You will need to hire an attorney—make sure yours is considered reputable. It is wise to use a bilingual lawyer, for all documents must be written in Spanish. Negotiate a fee for the task, not by the hour.

If you are content to buy at most one three-quarter-acre piece of property and do not intend to use it for commercial purposes, your purchase will be relatively easy. Honduran law allows a foreigner to own land of that size or smaller in his own name.

If you buy from a developer, make sure your lot is surveyed and legally described. Get his written commitment to provide utilities and a road to your property by a certain time. If he is also overseeing construction, insist on a schedule of completion.

If you are buying directly from the owner of the land, your attorney must conduct a title search. Searches should be especially strenuous if you are buying waste land from a municipality. At present, title insurance is not available in Honduras. You'll also need a good survey and description of your lot. Don't settle in before your attorney signals that all is clear.

You can expect to pay at least 6 percent in closing costs and transfer taxes. If a broker has brought you together with the seller, he will expect a commission. A Realtor's commission of about 10 percent should be paid by the seller. It is best to clarify these matters in advance.

To purchase a tract of land larger than 3,000 square meters (nearly three-quarters of an acre), whether for personal or commercial purposes, you must form a corporation, either a limited partnership or a stock corporation, the latter generally preferred as simpler.

Although the corporation must have at least five shareholders, they need do nothing. By recent law you can be full owner of that corporation and control all the stock. Theoretically, as a corporation, you face no restrictions on building or developing your land.

If there are no extraordinary circumstances, it will take about eight days to form the corporation, issue your shares, and get your ID card, which will enable you to buy the land. All expenses, including those for an attorney, registration, and incorporation fees, should not exceed $1,800.

In land purchases of any size, once the survey and title search are declared satisfactory, your lawyer will file either an *escritura pública* or a *dominio pleno*. The former attests that ownership of the property has been verified and publicly filed as a transfer of property. The latter avers that no prior ownership has been recorded, in which case a judge must decide whether to grant ownership to the petitioner.

Notice of intended sale is posted for 30 days, during which the judge will talk to surrounding landowners and review relevant records. He then decides whether to issue the *dominio pleno* (full ownership). The new document is then stamped with the court's registry number and is publicly registered. If the purchase involves commitment to build, the promised building must be completed within three years or the purchaser will face fines.

In all these matters—buying, building, and investing—this book is only a general guide. For further instruction, I recommend *Honduras: The Owner's Manual*, published by *International Living*, for its 50-odd pages of detailed text and hundreds of pages of appendices. For investment questions, consult FIDE, San Pedro's Chamber of Commerce, or Honduras's Ministry of Economy and Commerce in Tegucigalpa.

12

▽△▽

Investment and
Work in Honduras

Honduras is in desperate need of foreign investment. Its gross national product is less than $9.5 billion. In 1994 its per capita income was estimated to be $630 per year. Foreign debt is staggering. Honduras is presently obligated to pay more than $200 million annually toward its debts. Despite austerity measures, the Honduran government spends more than it takes in. Trade, too, is imbalanced: Honduras imports—principally from the United States but also from Japan, Mexico, and Venezuela—about 12 percent more than it exports. Chief exports include machinery and transport equipment, chemical products, finished textiles, fuel and oil, and foodstuffs, mainly bananas, coffee, shrimp, lobster, and beef. Its urban unemployment rate has reached as high as 50 percent.

Only recently has the country begun to attract foreign investors. In 1990 Honduras began tearing down hampering investment restrictions, granting inviting tax exemptions, creating new free zones, and actively assisting new endeavors.

Growing Industries

The newly calm international scene encouraged the apparel piece-work industry, to give just one example. Between 1991 and 1995 the value of apparel exports to the United States sextupled. In the past six years the *maquilas* (factories) have created 60,000 new jobs. Although the pay is not good—piecework rates are allowed—the workers seem grateful for the steady employment. Koreans and Taiwanese are frequent investors, and such well-known American companies as Kmart, Fruit of the Loom, Oshkosh, Wrangler, and Red Cap Uniforms have factories in Honduras. And the Central American market, currently 20 million potential customers strong, is growing stronger by the day.

Companies are enjoying the exemptions and tax advantages of the Export Processing Zones: no taxes, no customs duties on materials you import or products you export as long as you remain within the zone, and no restrictions on the use of foreign exchange or repatriation of capital or profits. Plants set up by United Technologies, Maytag, Phelps-Dodge, IBM, and other firms enjoy these benefits. In exchange, the companies bring relatively decent pay and good working conditions to thousands of Honduran workers.

If you are a Daddy Warbucks investor, export processing zones offer a multitude of possibilities. The furniture export business is one such possibility. Rosewood, teak, and tropical walnut are commonly made into furniture by

James D. Gollin

Shrimping boats in Roatán

skilled Honduran artisans practicing their century-old craft. And Honduras is the third largest exporter of finished furniture—some in fine mahogany, most in strong Honduran pine—to the United States.

The presence of the largest cultivated shrimp farm in the Americas and an abundance of exotic fruits and vegetables may entice a venture into the frozen or canned food industry. Foodstuffs still account for much of Honduras's income. Dole and Chiquita dominate fruit exports and are considered responsible and socially aware employers, providing medical and other benefits to their workers as well as improved income and working conditions. The Pan American Agricultural School is training Honduran workers in canning, pickling, and frozen-food preparation.

A variety of agricultural projects are open, especially when married to the national ecology. As a private venture with government

---

If you are interested in investment in Honduras write or call FIDE, the Foundation for Investments and Development of Exports, also known as the Industrial Development Group-Honduras. FIDE is a nonprofit group dedicated to nurturing the development of Honduras. It is the fastest and most efficient source of information on business opportunities and contacts.

FIDE OFFICES

2100 Ponce de Leon Blvd.
Suite 1175
Coral Gables, FL 33134
tel. (305) 444-3060, fax (305) 444-1610

In Honduras:
Tegucigalpa, tel. 232-9345, fax 239-0677
San Pedro Sula, tel. 566-3040, fax 557-2162

approval, Eric Anderson and a friend are reforesting an old cattle ranch on Roatán with more than 70,000 trees, including mahogany, cashew, teak, cedar, and coconut.

Honduras is currently trying to reactivate some of its long-abandoned mines—good news for investors with subterranean ventures on their minds. Geologists from the JAPEX Geoscience Institute of Japan are investigating potential oil reserves in the Honduran Mosquitia. If the investigation—scheduled to be finished in 1998—produces positive results, the information will be sold to companies interested in the petroleum sector. Contact Honduras's Natural Resources Ministry for more details.

Dollars and Cents

The following figures should give you an idea of the cost of creating an export business in Honduras: Rental of existing complexes within export processing zones costs between $3 and $5 per square foot per year. Rentals in free trade zones range between $2 and $3.50 per square foot per year. Current programs aim to complete 130 factory shells in new industrial parks by 1998.

Container shipping worldwide is done from any of the four Caribbean ports and the one Pacific port. A 40-foot container sent from Puerto Cortés to Miami, a 48-hour service, costs about $1,400. Airfreight to Miami costs $1.54 per kilogram (a bit over two pounds), but to Houston it's only 83 cents. Electricity, occasionally erratic or interrupted, is 110 volts nationwide at about 8 cents per kilowatt-hour. Voltages of 230 and 460 can also be provided.

A new investment law, established in 1992, is slowly helping to set countrywide standards and decrease the factionalism among bureaucracies. Some of the confusion and contradiction that the law intends to end stems from Honduras's traditional spoils system. When one of the two major parties wins over the other, all heads of the opposition must fall. All appointed heads and sub-heads of agencies and ministries are replaced by members of the victorious party. Since there is no real civil service machinery in Honduras, novices tend to come to the forefront just as the directors already in office begin to acquire a degree of professionalism. John Dupuis, editor of *Honduras Tips*, sees the problem as a major drawback to the country's development and hopes for the gradual growth of a civil service system.

The government has set minimum wages since 1974, but enforcement has generally been lax. The present bare minimum—ignoring all required "extras"—is about 34 cents an hour for a 44-hour week. With benefits, the official minimum wage is 48 cents an hour, though many Hondurans are working doggedly at half that rate. (In September 1997, the minimum wage in the United States became $5.15 per hour.)

A company that pays maximum benefits for holidays, vacations, bonuses, social security, and other payroll deductions, faces a fully loaded labor cost of 94 cents an hour. That figure, however, is calculated on the assumption that all possible bonuses and incentives have been earned by workers achieving a 100 percent efficiency rate with no absences. Multinational companies usually pay less than that, but more than the standard minimum wage. Banana companies have paid at the top of the wage scale but, by mechanizing some stages, have downsized their workforces and caused some labor unrest. In terms of lempiras, the Honduran worker has experienced a diminution of wages and buying power.

The country's new progressive labor legislation is widely flouted by many foreign entrepreneurs because the governing agencies have neither the money to impose the regulations nor assurance that the

MAJOR AND GROWING INVESTMENT AREAS

- apparel
- frozen and canned foods
- fruit growing
- forestry
- mining
- tourism
- cattle raising
- furniture
- leather goods and apparel
- schools for computer literacy and electronic technology

time is yet ripe for enforcement. Because some foreign companies have ignored the effects of Honduran inflation on their workers, strikes and work stoppages have occurred among the 20 percent of the workforce that is unionized.

Modest Investments

You can still invest if your available capital is relatively modest. Such ventures as hotels, apartment houses, restaurants, bed-and-breakfasts, amusement parks, Laundromats, or anything that seems designed to promote tourism and increase the comfort of tourists are reasonable considerations.

The Tourist Free Zone Law offers the same financial benefits as the Private Export Processing Zones Law. Your proposal will be carefully studied for environmental impact, then, if your project is accepted, you'll pay no Honduran income tax on your profits for 20 years. You won't have to pay the local 7 percent sales tax on the wood and building materials you buy. You will pay a 1 percent asset tax on the capital registered after you've been in business for two years. Since this law also permits the importation of motor vehicles, boats, and airplanes for use within the zone, it opens a way for the investor-resident to bring in his automobile duty-free, so long as it will be used in the tourist trade.

Female Investors

If you are a woman alone and intend to function as an investor, brace yourself for condescension and patronization—vestiges of the old machismo. It is becoming less intrusive, but you will hear dismaying stories. Bill Martin tells of a female graduate of West Point who entered the army in her native Honduras. She made so little headway in the Honduran military that she resigned her commission. Another Honduran woman earned an MBA in the States, then returned to her homeland to work for her father's business. He put her to work opening mail. She has since returned to the United States.

But times are changing. Women driving trucks and buses are no longer a novelty, nor are women owning and running independent businesses. Two English-language papers in Honduras are owned and run by women. Kenya Lima de Zapata directs tourism activities on the Bay Islands, and in the fall of 1997, Nora Gúnera de Melgar ran a strong race for the national presidency.

Work Residency

Should you choose to take a job rather than invest, a good attorney can obtain a work residency for you in three or four months, renewed every year for 250 lempiras at the immigration office. Naturally you will have to pay Honduran income tax but that amount can be deducted from your payment to the IRS. College-level teachers, scientists, and business consultants are courted and are readily granted work permits.

If you are much too young to retire but simply want to work at your métier in a new setting, advertise your specialty in one of the newspapers. Joe Wagner, who runs Caribbean Electrical in Roatán, tells me that skilled electricians, carpenters, and plumbers can almost write their own tickets on Roatán and in the mainland cities. All you need is a work visa or an ordinary visa with monthly renewals.

The trick in obtaining permission to work lies in your employer's insistence that you are not depriving a national of a job—that your skills cannot be found among the nationals in the area.

Taxes

Although most investors in the export processing zones and tourist projects are fully or partly exempt from paying taxes on their profits, earned income is of course subject to taxation.

The wage earner pays income tax on his Honduran income at the municipality office. There he will be asked his income and told the corresponding tax. Incomes between 20,000L and 50,000L ($1,500 and $3,800) are in the 12 percent bracket, and those between 50,000L and 100,000L ($3,800 and $7,600) are in the 14 percent bracket. The tax mounts incrementally. Earning more than one million lemps per year (about $76,000) puts you in the 34 percent area.

Hondurans and Work

It has been said that the mestizo Honduran values the pleasures of family, conversation, and friendship far more than the North American notion of "getting ahead." True, the work rhythms in Honduras are often more leisurely and relaxed than the dances. This can give some Americans pause, especially those planning to invest. The question naturally arises: If an investor's project is approved and his funds are adequate, will he find workers who will really work?

The answer is yes. In no way can Hondurans be considered averse to hard work. Indeed, for a cause they see as just and needful, they will work like the pyramid builders of ancient Egypt or the cathedral masons of the Middle Ages. The experience of Eric Anderson of the French Harbor Yacht Club is a fine example. Anderson had engineered the excavation of a great kidney-shaped hole into which a shaped-metal pool form would be inserted. When the time came to insert the form, he realized that vehicular access to the pit was blocked.

"No problem," his gang of workers assured him. They mounted the massive steel form on log rollers and towed it up a sidehill, around one of his newly constructed terraces. Once over the top, having detoured around the water tower, the form began to slip downhill, headed straight for the marina. "I thought it would surely land in the water," Anderson recalls, "and take a couple of boats with it. Or that I might have to fit it with an outboard motor and make it the largest and strangest motorboat launch in the islands. But some-how—I still don't know how they managed it—they blocked its slide, ramming some of the logs in front of it, and then levered it gently as you please into place." And there it now sits, a sparkling and refreshing pool. J. Peter Hughes, who runs a subsidiary of Maytag, also notes that Honduran workers, even those who are semiliterate, are easily trained.

The difficulty of the work is never a question. The focus is always on the time element. Jorge Brower, head of the Trujillo Bay Hotel, tells a very meaningful story in this regard. His first job, at age 13, was in a soap factory. Determined to make a good impression and secure his job, he worked like mad, exceeding everyone else's productivity by a wide margin.

After a week or two, the foreman called him in for a private conference. Jorge was aghast. "What is it, sir? Is it that my work is poor?" "No," was the answer. "You do very good work." "What then is wrong," Jorge understandably wanted to know. "You work well," answered the foreman, "but you work too fast." He went on to explain that theirs was a small factory with a limited market. They made exactly as many bars of soap as they could sell. And that amount of work provided employment to all the able-bodied workers in the pueblo. Jorge was disrupting the natural rhythm of the work.

Although good at what they do, Honduran laborers, including the foremen, require supervision. In his interpretation of your plans and specifications, the foreman may be extraordinarily imaginative or stubbornly insistent on traditional ways, especially in building projects. If you are not regularly present to check on every step, the house you get, according to one veteran resident, "is not what you expect, but what you inspect."

Of course, thievery exists even in idyllic countries, but a stern code of honor and honesty has deep roots even among the poorest of the poor. The housemaid departing for a brief holiday among her people traditionally opens her traveling bag and displays its contents to the mistress of the house before leaving. Lou Shimkin tells of a maid's persistence in this practice for years, even though he and his wife have assured her that they have perfect trust in her. The time-honored habit stands.

The Right Manager for the Job

If you come from a career in management and wish to invest in Honduras, you might consider buying an existing company that suffers for lack of the financial or managerial skills you possess. That advice comes from Henrik Jensen, a polyglot entrepreneur on Utila. He claims that a number of suitable locations, and prospective markets, are failing from the top down. They need skilled and resourceful management.

Before taking such a step, Jensen counsels, the managerial candidate should honestly analyze his own temperament, flexibility, and sensitivity to the needs of others, especially subordinates. The successful captain of an American enterprise is not always a capable pilot of a Honduran venture. He may be fluent in Spanish but tongue-tied in empathy.

"Perhaps the most important prerequisite for the prospective investor is analysis of his or her own temperament. Autocrats need not apply."

Autocrats need not apply. Jim Davis, expatriate entrepreneur of Trujillo, warns that some Americans project an attitude of superiority and condescension. But the manager who barks may get bitten. Curt commands and abrasive manners clash with Ladino *personalismo*. Public berating of inefficient or blundering employees is unforgivable. A private dressing-down is not much of an improvement. The recipient feels degraded and dishonored, and honor is his dearest possession.

According to Helen Murphy, an experienced manager of macho Hondurans, now a Realtor in La Ceiba, the best approach is not accusation but discussion. Managers might ask: "What would you feel about this problem if you were in my shoes?" or "Can you think of a way we can improve this situation?" The Honduran responds much more favorably to a request for help or a challenge to change than to scowls or threats.

The business dynamo who tries to remold his subordinates will find his Honduran workers smiling but unchanged. High-pressure types find it difficult to accept a mañana country, according to Eric Anderson, owner of the French Harbor Yacht Club on Roatán. "You can beat your head against a wall until you accept that this is a different pace of life. Every year people come down here to show us how to do it. They usually don't last. From experience, I've learned that instead of pushing gung ho at one project, I'll have three or four going at once and try to advance that way."

The Honduran worker knows well the sweat of hard labor but not the cold sweat of frenzy and haste. Of course, Hondurans recognize time, but on them it does not exercise the imperious demands it does on us. About 30 years ago, Herman Wouk described the attitude of the entire Caribbean area when he spoke of a "wisdom" that a climate of eternal summer teaches. "It is that, under all the parade of human effort and noise, today is like yesterday, and tomorrow will be like today, that existence is a wheel of recurring patterns from which no one escapes, that all anybody does in life is live for a while and then die for good, without finding out much; and that therefore the idea is to take things easy and enjoy the passing time under the sun. The white people have . . . come before and gone before."[1]

---

1. Herman Wouk, *Don't Stop the Carnival* (Garden City, N.Y.: Doubleday, 1965) 5.

13

Planning Your First Trip

Honduras is a place where many retirees have found pleasurable retirement, and some investors have found a profitable financial adventure. If you are thinking seriously of either possibility, you should plan before your first trip.

Your first trip to the country might well be with a tour. If you speak no Spanish, the tour is probably advisable. Don't hesitate to ask about the backgrounds of the guides who will conduct your tour. I once had an "English-speaking" guide whose English I found to be unintelligible. I list a number of possible tour groups in the back of this book and on page 108.

Be sure to ask specific questions about accommodations and get a copy of the itinerary in advance. Take a tour that offers you at least ten days or preferably two weeks.

While on the tour, learn as much as possible about making telephone calls, reservations, purchases, and the like, so you'll be confident enough to make your next trip on your own.

If you have self-confidence, a spirit of adventure, and at least a

▼▲▼

smattering of traveler's Spanish, you may want to create your own trip to suit your chief interests and inclinations.

If you are a devotee of aquatic sports and see beaches in your future, the Bay Islands should occupy most of your trip, with emphasis on Roatán. Also be sure to visit Guanaja and Utila and the mainland North Coast, especially Trujillo and La Ceiba. Your travel agent should be able to find you an air-hotel package for the islands for only a little more than you'd pay for air travel alone.

If you are thinking of a simple and relaxed life in retirement, don't neglect Siguatepeque or La Esperanza, roughly halfway between San Pedro and Tegucigalpa. You will certainly need some Spanish in these towns.

If you have any interest in the Mayan mystery, a guided tour of the ruins and an inexpensive overnight stay in the charming colonial town of Copán can be easily arranged in San Pedro Sula. Be sure to check out prices and promises with at least two tour companies.

For official business, Tegucigalpa is the center of government, although most departments and bureaus also have branches in San Pedro Sula. Make afternoon appointments as early as possible—it's a rare government office that is open after 4 p.m. Early closings are especially likely on Fridays.

Air Travel

If you plan to arrive by air, your minimum needs are a round-trip ticket and your passport. Because Latin American countries change their rules from time to time, a call to the nearest Honduran consulate is advisable. Canada has consulates in Montreal and Ottawa. The United States has seven besides the embassy in Washington.

Frequently, visitors who don't arrive with a tour group are asked to show their return-trip tickets as assurance that they won't wind up as public charges. Don't buy your return flight in Honduras. Not only are there steep fares for one-way travel but there are also heavy taxes and no senior citizen discounts for foreign travelers.

A valid passport issued by the United States, Canada, most western European countries, most Central and South American countries, or Japan is sufficient. Visas are not required for U.S. citizens. (Citizens of other countries may need to ask for a visa at the nearest Honduran consulate.) For $2, an entry stamp or ticket will be placed in your passport, good for 30 days and renewable.

If you've lost your passport or have not yet been issued one, you can gain entry on a tourist card, sold for $2 at airline check-in counters. You'll need proof of citizenship in your home country. (If you are using your passport, check the expiration date before leaving; travelers occasionally forget to renew in ample time.)

Airlines servicing Honduras are listed in the "Communications and Transportation" chapter. Since you are flying internationally, remember to confirm your reservations 72 hours before your flight and to check-in two hours before takeoff. If cost is a consideration, avoid flying during the peak-fare season, usually June through September. Midweek travel is usually cheaper than weekend. APEX fares (advance purchases, usually three weeks ahead of time) are less expensive and often allow you "open-jaw" reservations (arrival and departure from different cities).

It is usually costly to ask for an open return date. If you do decide to outstay your return date, the airlines commonly charge about $60 to change the reservation, much less than the extra fee for an open-return ticket.

If you intend to visit Mexico or a Latin American country besides Honduras, you may find it advantageous to fly with one of the smaller regional airlines. For Canadians, a direct flight to Cancún offers easy access to Honduras. A round trip between Yucatán and San Pedro Sula only costs about $200. Such small airlines as Copa, Isleña, and Aviateca, as well as the larger Lacsa and Taca, often offer great bargains. For a multicountry jaunt to at least three destinations for a modest price, call the Visit Central America Program, (800) 255-8222.

Other Modes of Travel

If you are also visiting Guatemala, El Salvador, or Nicaragua, it is possible to reach Honduras by bus. The trip is very economical but not recommended. Border crossings are usually allowed only during daylight hours, and border regions are often dangerous. For up-to-date information on the safety of such regions, call (202) 647-5225 for the State Department's emergency hotline.

I do not recommend driving down in a car, especially for your first trip. But if you do, you'll need to show documents for the car as well as your driver's license. And if it's a rented car, be sure that the contract expressly allows for international travel.

Entrance by your own boat is not only possible but exhilarating, if you have ample time and are starting from the Caribbean. The easiest objective is probably the island of Roatán. The customs office is at Coxen Hole, which serves as the island's capital. You can find agreeable mooring at the French Harbor Yacht Club or on the opposite side of the island at the pricier Anthony's Key Resort. See the back of this book for some pertinent publications.

If you'd prefer to arrive by small plane, there are many small airstrips in all sorts of unlikely places. These are relics of the Contra years, and Honduras has more than any other Central American country. For many well-to-do residents the private plane was the preferred mode of travel before Honduras awoke to its need for decent roads. But you may not land a private plane on the jet field at Roatán. La Ceiba is your proper target.

Packing and Supplies

One secret of successful travel is to take as little as possible—only what is absolutely needed. Portability usually eases and speeds

TRAVEL TIPS

- Exchange U.S.dollars in Honduras for a better rate.
- Carry cash and credit cards in a pouch on belt or a money purse worn lavaliere style under shirt.
- Tip bellhops, porters, and chambermaids from $1 to $2.
- Don't tip cab drivers unless a special service has been included.

arrivals and departures. Generally speaking, two light suitcases are preferable to one heavy one. Even if you are traveling first class, there will be times when you won't have a porter.

If you bring your own diving equipment, make sure you have good locks, additional taping, colorful markings, and labels on the equipment and cases. Keep a wary eye on your gear's delivery, especially in the arrival sheds of regional airlines. Watch the unloading of the cargo bays of small airplanes for fear of careless oversight as much as theft.

Pack whatever medications you may need. Sunscreen (SPF 15 minimum) and insect repellent are also necessities, but you need not pack a large amount for both are widely available in Honduras. Adhesive bandages and small bottles of antiseptic and analgesics (stomach soothers) round out the medical supplies. (You need not overdo medical preparations—see the "Health and Medicine" chapter.) Bring sunglasses and, if you wear glasses or contact lenses, bring an extra pair.

When packing toiletries, consider bulk and weight. Take sample sizes of toothpaste, deodorant, shaving cream, lotions, depilatories, and the like. Plug-ins like electric shavers and hair dryers work in Honduran outlets.

Other bring-alongs include a camera and film. Film is much cheaper in the States; avid shutterbugs may wish to bring a number of rolls of film in a lead-lined bag (purchased at any large camera store). If you're taking a camcorder, put any exposed film in the lead bag also. X-ray machines tend to wipe out the recording. Also, don't leave your camera or film on dashboards or any place where they'll be exposed to the hot sun. Your camera lens may warp and your film may acquire a purple tone.

A small flashlight may be useful because power outages do occur. Sports equipment that responds only to your touch is OK, but you should probably forget the golf clubs. Golf courses are few in Honduras.

What to Wear

Wardrobe selection is the inexperienced traveler's Waterloo. A good rule: Take more money and less clothing than you think you'll need.

You are going to the tropics. Take no winter wear even if you freeze in the taxi to your home airport. Avoid extremes in your choice of swimwear. Honduras is neither a nunnery nor playboy resort, although some beaches have no taboos. In clothes the emphasis should be on lightweight and wash-and-wear. Cottons and synthetic blends are best. Four complete changes should suffice.

Lightweight slacks and long-sleeved shirts or blouses are helpful at insect-ridden beaches, and you'll need a sweater or jacket in the mountainous areas, like Tegucigalpa, where the nights are cool. Allow yourself one dressy skirt or, for men, one featherweight sports coat, a light pair of slacks, and a tie if you expect to do much business in the capital. One very light but sturdy raincoat or poncho is also needed.

Informality of dress is the norm. Neither coat nor tie is required even in government offices. A guayabera shirt, worn untucked, is equally acceptable. Shorts are accepted everywhere. Running shoes are common, and the nonskid soles are practical on boats. Add a light sweater for cool nights in the mountains and a sun hat or visored cap, and your wardrobe is complete.

> "A good rule:
> Take more money
> and less clothing
> than you think
> you'll need."

The secret to fresh clean clothes lies in one-day laundry and ironing services available almost everywhere for pennies. The results are good, but you might not want to surrender a very lacy or delicate blouse, since it may be beaten clean on rocks in a nearby stream. If you rinse out items by hand, remember that nothing dries overnight on the North Coast or along the gulf during the rainy season.

Customs

In Honduras the lack of uniformity of regulations is endemic and necessitates hesitant dashes and seeming contradictions. Your entry stamp—or stapled ticket—which may or may not cost you about $2—is good for 90 days. It's renewable for 30 days at a time at any immigration office or some banks for $1. The total continuous stay, whether you entered on a consular visa or simply your passport, is 180 days. If you wish to stay longer, you must leave the country—over the border near Copán into Guatemala will do. You must stay outside three days—or only overnight according to some adventurers—before reentering for another maximum of 180 days. These restrictions apply if you enter as a visitor, the appropriate status for your first trip.

You may bring in anything reasonable for a vacation. Personal electronic gadgets and items intended as gifts are allowed if they are worth under $1,000. (This allowance may have changed; check before leaving.) Don't bring any fresh fruits or vegetables, even if they're only intended for personal consumption. Firearms are frowned on; if you must bring one, be sure you have your Honduran consular permit, obtained in advance. Pets also require advance permission, often a tedious process. Cats can be troublesome because Hondurans don't usually regard cats as pets, and cat food is hard to find in Honduras.

James D. Gollin

Copán, the site of Mayan ruins, is a popular tourist spot.

You may import two liters of alcohol and 200 cigarettes or 50 cigars from duty-free shops. However, I wouldn't bother. The native rum, beer, cigars, and cigarettes are good and about one-third their cost back home. Liquor that must be imported anyway, like Scotch whiskey, is a duty-free bargain because it will cost twice as much in Honduras as in the States.

Guarding Against Theft

While Honduras is probably safer than its neighbors, certain precautions against theft should be taken any time you travel. To safeguard your passport and credit card, both golden targets for thieves, I recommend the purchase of a money belt or pouch, worn under your clothes either lavaliere style or clipped to your belt. Camping stores offer a variety of these. It is best to leave expensive necklaces and chains at home, and don't carry excessive amounts of cash when sightseeing (most hotels have a safe-deposit box).

Purses are best worn with a strap over the shoulder. Never carry valuables in the outside pocket of a coat or in the hip pocket of trousers. A hip pocket is easily sliced with a razor and emptied without any telltale pressure. Pickpockets often work in pairs—one distracts, the other steals.

Reminders About Money

Ideally, your money should be in traveler's checks in U.S. dollars. In the bigger cities, Canadian dollars, English pounds, and German marks can be exchanged, but usually at an unfavorable rate. In addition, it is advisable to have some U.S. cash in ones and fives. They come in handy for entry and exit fees, your first currency exchange, tipping, and occasional unexpected needs. A credit card is also a good idea. Visa, MasterCard, and American Express are generally accepted and can be used for car rentals, posh restaurants, and upscale hotels.

At the airport *cambio*, exchange only a small amount. Instead, look for the *casas de cambio* and banks advertised in *Honduras This Week*. Convert your traveler's checks there. Your hotel will also change money but usually not as favorably. Make sufficient exchanges on weekdays to last over the weekend. Keep those few spare bills in American money handy. Should you run out of Honduran cash, your credit cards offer a limited solution. And as your time of departure draws near, cut down your exchanges markedly, leaving yourself enough for only departure taxes and gifts because the reverse exchange, lempiras to dollars, can be tricky and slightly painful.

On your return to the United States, your departure tax, collected at the airline counter in Honduras, will be about $16. You have a U.S. exemption of $600 on your Honduran purchases, including a quart of alcohol and 200 cigarettes. Be sure not to take

out any pre-Columbian articles and resist coral and shell tempta-
tions. These could be confiscated and create a legal stew.

If you are budgeting somewhat closely, figure that you will pay a
7 percent sales tax on most goods and services, 10 percent on your
bar bills, and 2.5 percent on your regional airline tickets.

Tipping

Understandably, Americans are expected to tip. But the extreme
roles of Lady Bountiful and Scrooge should be avoided. A favorable
exchange rate should not provoke showers of lempiras. Such behav-
ior demeans the national currency as play money and the recipient as
a menial, while feeding inflation of expectations. Both Belize and
Costa Rica have suffered on this account. For a complete discussion
of this issue, see the "Money Matters" chapter.

Your tips to bellhops, porters, and chambermaids will probably
range from $1 to $2. For cab rides, almost no one tips. Pay the pre-
arranged amount unless an extra service is provided. For other services for which you would tip in the States, tip at about half of the
stateside amount.

Holidays

If you intend to do any serious research in government offices or make
any major purchases, you should be aware of Honduran holidays,
listed on page 186. On the most important of these holidays you won't
find a single bank, tour office, or airlines reservation counter open for
business. You may not be able to rent a car or book a tour. Four of
these holidays are less important: the Day of the Americas and the
three that fall in October. On these you may find some businesses
open. Easter is a movable holy day, coming on the first Sunday after
the first full moon after the first day of spring. Some businesses take
off all of Holy Week (the week before Easter).

Almost every town has a special festival date, usually honoring a
patron saint but sometimes a local product, like the potato festival in
La Esperanza in July. Not much serious business takes place during

▼▲▼▲▼▲▼▲▼▲▼▲▼▲▼▲▼▲▼▲▼▲▼▲▼▲▼▲▼▲▼▲▼▲▼▲▼

festivals. Drink, feasts, parades, dances, and costumed processions abound. If you wish to witness any festivals during your visit, you can match them to your itinerary by asking the Honduran Institute of Tourism for their *Listado General de las Ferias, Festivales y Otras Celebraciónes.*

Stores and businesses owned by Seventh-Day Adventists are closed on Saturday (the Sabbath) but may open briefly after sunset and also on Sunday morning. In hot regions of the coast, most businesses keep only morning hours (8 to 11 a.m.) on Saturday. If you intend a noontime visit to any commercial establishment on any weekday, it's wise to call ahead. Many businesses and even some small banks close for a couple of hours in the heat of the day. Most close between noon and 1 p.m. or maintain very limited service.

The Bay Islands

Roatán

Chances are, the first stop on your Honduran tour will be the Bay Island of Roatán. Once you settle in, orient yourself quickly by visiting

▼▲▼▲▼▲▼▲▼▲▼▲▼▲▼▲▼▲▼▲▼▲▼▲▼▲▼▲▼▲▼▲▼▲▼▲▼

HONDURAN HOLIDAYS

New Year's Day	January 1
Day of the Americas	April 14
Easter	Good Friday to following Sunday
Labor Day	May 1
Independence Day	September 15
Francisco Morazán Day	October 3
Columbus Day (Dìa de la Raza)	October 12
Armed Forces Day	October 21
Christmas Eve and Christmas	December 24–25
New Year's Eve	December 31

▲▼▲▼▲▼▲▼▲▼▲▼▲▼▲▼▲▼▲▼▲▼▲▼▲▼▲▼▲▼▲▼▲▼▲▼▲

Coxen Hole, the slightly dingy village that serves as the capital, less than a mile west of the airport.

Stop in at the Librería Casi Todo (Almost Everything Bookstore). This shop offers not only all manner of periodicals, maps, and informative publications but also a warm welcome by owner Pat Wagner. (She also runs a travel agency that can arrange all your island and mainland travel.) Sip a cappuccino or munch a sandwich while you browse. Ask Pat about the glass-bottom boat trips and whether Tim Bolton's beautiful half-hour video on diving off Roatán is on sale yet. (Or contact Tim himself through the Mermaid Tavern at Brick Bay, just up the road to the east.) The bookstore offers copies of *Honduras This Week* and *Honduras Tips*, both in English and your scriptures for getting around Honduras. You might also pick up a funny and perceptive commentary on language difficulties, *Wee Speak*, by Candace Hammond.

At the same spot you can also buy the magazine specific to Roatán, the *Coconut Telegraph*, but I recommend that you go instead to the publication's offices in downtown Coxen Hole and introduce yourself to the amiable editor-publisher Marion Seaman. A humane dynamo, she knows all the residents and is always organizing groups for the improvement of the island she clearly loves. In the *Telegraph* you'll find two indispensable maps: one of Roatán and another outlining the major Bay Islands.

While in Coxen Hole you can change money at three banks at a better rate than those usually offered at hotels, make long-distance calls easily at the Hondutel offices, and check prices at the town's two supermarkets, Warren's and Eldon's. Although seafood, local products, and groceries seem inexpensive, all but the seafood has to fold in shipping costs from the mainland. (The same items on the mainland are usually 10 to 20 percent cheaper, in part because mainland retailers figure on a lower profit margin than those on the resort islands.) If you're hungry, Warren's diner-type restaurant serves up a chicken dinner for $3.

If you plan to spend time diving on Roatán, remember to take your PADI or SSI certification card. The resorts insist on it. The more luxurious resort hotels have their own dive shops, the cost of which is factored into the price of your stay. They make everything easy: Your equipment and compressors are waiting for you at the dock.

You can enjoy a week of diving for about half to two-thirds of what you would pay in Belize. Full equipment rental will run around $40 per day. Resorts and shops supply air tanks, weights, guides, and boats. If you're a beginner staying without a diving package, dozens of dive shops will offer to introduce you to the sport for about $35 to $75. Full courses are also very reasonably priced. Certification usually takes about four days of instruction.

Snorkeling also offers dazzling sights. You can rent fins and masks for only a few dollars per day. If you are new to snorkeling, be sure your mask fits tightly. Try rented equipment underwater before venturing out. If you have a mustache, you may have leakage around your upper lip. A liberal application of lip balm can create a snug fit. The Blue Channel on the west end of Roatán is said to be especially rewarding for snorkelers.

You can rent a car, van, or motorcycle at Coxen Hole or at the airport—something you can't do on Guanaja or Utila. Unlike the other islands, Roatán is drivable almost its entire length. Taxis are everywhere, collective in ridership, and inexpensive: for $1 to $5 you can go anywhere. Buses run about every half hour on weekdays, east or west from Coxen Hole. You can rent bicycles for $1 per hour or less, but the island is hilly and not necessarily an easy ride. For saddle horses, ask around at French Harbor. Kayaks, canoes, Windsurfers, and paddleboats can also be rented at several places on the island.

Two Roatán towns are particularly pleasant to stroll through. Oak Ridge, near the East End, is picturesque and very Caribbean with a lively harbor. West End, geographically named, offers long sandy beaches, young travelers in high spirits, a variety of shops— many showcasing native arts and crafts—and an air of *mañana* spiced with *dolce far niente*. A taxi to either destination from Coxen Hole costs just over $5, less if you pick up other travelers.

Naturally you'll want to see the Garifunas at Punta Gorda. A tour group called Island Adventures will escort you by boat through mangrove mazes and tropical gardens, and top it off with a Garifuna dance performance. Or you can go on your own initiative with new-found friends on a Saturday evening.

Sandy Bay offers two attractions. The **Carambola Botanical Gardens** are a breathtaking botanical binge. For a $4 fee the **Roatán Museum and Institute for the Marine Sciences** at Anthony's Key Resort offers dioramas of the colonial period, a number of pre-Columbian artifacts, and a dolphin show. You can dive and swim with the dolphins for sizable added fees of $75 or $100.

A wonderfully friendly place for a drink, good conversation, and a chance to meet expatriates is the **Mermaid Tavern** in Brick Bay. With luck you might meet John Davies there, the premier island historian and raconteur of grueling and ghastly snippets of the island's piratical past.

Because many hotels wrap meals and diving packages into their overall price, it's a good idea to get a travel agent who is a good negotiator. If you wish to negotiate directly, ask if taxes and service charges are included. If you don't wish to have diving privileges, be

Anthony's Key Resort is a Roatán favorite.

sure to make that clear. The price will vary with the number in your group and the season, summer and fall being the cheapest.

Resort-level hotels are pricey and cater to the affluent—they can run well over $100 per day per person. However, compared to places like Acapulco and Cancún they may seem moderate. Unless otherwise indicated, credit cards are accepted.

Anthony's Key Resort (tel. 445-1003) includes in its price, about $240 a day with diving, a gorgeous setting, three hearty buffet-style meals a day, visits to the museum and the dolphin show, tennis, picnics, horseback rides, and activities with a variety of watercraft.

Fantasy Island Beach Resort (reservations, 800-676-2826) really on a little islet, offers 76 lavish rooms with air-conditioning, generous bathrooms, and private balconies for $100 per night per person including meals.

Coco View Resort (tel. 445-1013), dedicated to diving, can also supply information about the possibility of renting a house at Playa Miguel, the next-door development.

Paya Bay Resort (tel. 665-2139), a creation of two individualists, Lurlene and Mervin McNab, sits on a cliff on the northeast corner of the island and offers views of both sides. The resort is near a promontory known as "Alligator's Nose," a fair drive from the airport into the "unfashionable" East End. The McNabs will pick you up at the airport then drive you over a bumpy dirt road to a lush, bird-filled forest and the set of terraced buildings that make up the resort. One of the buildings includes a charming dining room that looks like a medieval Italian baptistery. The "American Plan" (food included) runs $100 for a single or $60 per person in a double. A stay here offers a chance to explore land for sale in the much more affordable East End.

French Harbor Yacht Club (tel. 445-1478), a five-minute walk from the town of French Harbor, is a friendly and affordable hilltop spot. Its kidney-shaped pool, as well as its decks and terraces—one with a waterfall—seem to slope into the marina where about 20 boats of varying size are sheltered. Fax and laundry services are available, and efficiency apartments are under construction.

If for business reasons you wish to stay a day or two in Coxen Hole, you might try the **Hotel Cay View Resort** (tel. 445-1202), the best hotel in that crowded little town. The resort is unpretentious but clean and has a terrace from which you can enjoy the view of the cay and watch cruise-ship tourists step ashore. Simple and basic, it has an acceptable bar and restaurant, but its chief virtue is location. No meals are included in the low price (about $40 for a double), and no credit cards are accepted.

West End restaurants are generally inexpensive. **Cabinas a Orillas del Mar** is noted for its banana pancakes and good omelets. **Vivian and Foster's** provides honest sandwich lunches. At dinnertime the airy restaurant at **Half Moon Bay Cabins** does pleasant things with shrimp. **Oceanside Inn** in Sandy Bay features American-style seafood, and the **French Harbor Yacht Club** has good variety and even bakes quiches at lunch. In Coxen's Hole try the restaurants at **Hotel Sheila** and **Hotel El Paso**, or check the authenticity of the **Burger Hut**. If you get to Punta Gorda, **Ben Gonzalez** has a dive shop, cabins, a bar, and a café where you can sample about eight different "typical" foods, shrimp prepared six different ways, and honey-glazed lobster tails. Remember to drink only bottled water unless the hotel or restaurant assures you that the water they serve is purified and free of *turista*.

When you are ready to leave, you will probably fly. There is very cheap boat service—ask at Coxen Hole—but the local airlines, Isleña, Sosa, and Caribbean Air, offer such quick and inexpensive trips among the islands and the nearby mainland city of La Ceiba that you'll waste vacation time if you don't take them. Sosa has direct flights to Guanaja.

Guanaja

Arriving by air on this beautiful forested island, you will land on a small airstrip on the edge of the canal that cuts the island about a third of the way from its southwestern tip. Ignore the Hotel Hillton—it's no relation to the North American Hilton and is best left to airline personnel who need proximity to the airstrip. Except for beaches and the capital, Bonacca, on a tiny cluster of islets offshore, the runway, terminal, and dock area are the last expanse of level land you're likely to see on this island. But not the last smiles.

▼▲▼

If Roatán seemed friendly, Guanaja is even warmer, perhaps because it sees fewer tourists.

If you are booked at one of the luxury resorts, they will send a boat to meet you. Make sure arrangements are made for pickup; otherwise a water taxi for the 20- or 30-minute trip to any of the resorts will cost you at least $10.

On this island I would advise you—even if you have no intention of diving—to ignore the expense factor and reserve a room at one of the resorts. They are lavish but worth the cost to keep the vacation spirit alive. Although classy as accommodations go, they do not have air conditioning. Ceiling fans and constant sea breezes do the trick.

There are at least three delightful resorts, costing between $200 and $300 per couple with meals and two or three dives included per day. Non-diving guests can hope for a 15 to 20 percent reduction. An interesting diving target on the south side is the *Jado Trader*, a deliberately sunken wreck resting under about 30 years of sea.

Posada del Sol (Inn of the Sun; tel. 453-4311 or in the United States 800-642-3483) is a Spanish colonial–style building housing 23 bright rooms with beamed ceilings, large louvered windows, and tile floors. Palm trees and bougainvillea hem the hardwood deck around the pool and adjoining thatched-roof bar, tennis court, workout room, and gift shop. The small beach next to the dock offers shore fishing as well as waterskiing and windsurfing. Captain Terry is the attentive manager.

Bayman Bay Club (in the United States 800-524-1823) offers elegance in the midst of a jungle. For about $250 per couple per day—less if you're not a diver—you are housed in individual cottages on a hill overlooking a pleasant little beach and a 100-yard dock. Besides diving and kayaking, the resort offers fine buffet dining, picnics, and excursions. The clubhouse has a bar, billiard table, reading corner, and observation deck.

Nautilus Resort (tel. 237-0397 or in the United States 800-535-7063), renovated and upgraded a few years ago, decorates its six rooms in Mexican and Central American styles but with TVs and VCRs and with balconies from which you can see Bonacca, convenient if you have business there. Non-divers pay about $130 per couple per day. Horseback riding, fishing, and sailing are available.

If you find Guanaja enthralling and contemplate settling down there, the official you should contact is the vivacious Kenya Lima de Zapata, the mayor's wife and the Department of Tourism's *jefe regional* of the Bay Islands. You would also do well to reach Jack Midence, an engineer who divides his time between his development on 25 acres of Sandy Bay in Guanaja and Sisco International, a construction firm in Tegucigalpa. *International Living* recommends Guanaja Properties as Realtors.

For a few dollars you can take a water taxi from the airstrip to the island's capital town of Guanaja (also called Bonacca or El Cayo by its residents). Much of the town has the look of an old black-and-white frontier movie set.

The town's main street is truly main, crowded with the services the visitor needs. The Sosa office will arrange flights to Roatán for about $14 or to La Ceiba on the mainland for about $17. **Bancahsa** and **Banco Atlántida** take care of currency exchange. Hondutel and the post office face each other. The supermarket, **Casa Sikaffy**, a bit farther along, is open every day. Down a side street is a basic clinic, **Centro de Salud**, with an English-speaking staff.

Lodgings here are plain and basic, quite different from the island's resorts. If business requires you to stay over, two possibilities are the accommodating but rather dark **Hotel Miller** (tel. 453-4327) and the **Hotel Alexander** (tel. 453-4326), where some rooms face the sea. Both have double rooms with private bath, air conditioning, and cable television for $30 to $35 per night. Meals are not included, nor are credit cards accepted. Weekly and monthly rates are extremely low. For a few dollars more try Bo Bush's **Island House** on the north side. It's ideal for short stays, and prices include three meals and beach access. Inquire at the Sosa office.

The locals find food and drink at **Glenda's, Bahia Resort, The Silver Dollar,** and **Ca Fé Coral.** Less expensive—about $3 for dinner—are **Café Bonacco** in a corner of the supermarket and **Joe's**, in the middle of town. You can dance to jukebox music at the **Mountain View** overlooking the water.

Utila

Utila is only 22 miles from the mainland city of La Ceiba. The ferry makes the 90-minute ride for about $6, or a plane does the same in 15 minutes for about $15.

Two-thirds of the island is a mangrove swamp adjoining a beautiful lagoon with a hemline of dry land on one side. Planes land on an airstrip of pressed earth and stone at the edge of the island's only town. (The tarmac was originally paved but, because seawater was mixed with the cement, the surface crumbled.)

A pickup truck meets all flights and provides taxi service to all diving service hotels and guest houses, although they're all just a short walk away down one of the island's two roads. If you haven't booked a place to stay, and there's room, the truck will take you along for a dollar.

The town's main street, a two-lane paved strip barely wide enough for two passenger cars to edge past each other, runs for a little less than a mile to East Harbor. The road is lined by pretty but unpretentious clapboard houses with Victorian facades. There are no

Guanaja's major town is built mostly over water.

James D. Gollin

sidewalks, so pedestrians stroll along the road while bicyclists weave around them.

The thoroughfare's only cross-street will take you to Bancahsa and nearby Banco Atlántida, waiting to cash your checks. The **Casino** disco is across from the bank. A number of dive shops are nearby, as are the post office, police station, and **Hondutel**. Fronting the small park abutting the main street is the **Community Clinic**, useful only for very minor emergencies.

For exercise, you can walk in the park or hire a bike for 50 cents an hour or $3 per day. If you'd prefer to get your workout on the water, kayaks, paddleboats, and even dugouts can be rented. Tourist information is available at the **Tour and Travel Center**, next door to the **Mermaid's Corner**, a good place for lunch.

The **Pumpkin Hill** area is worth investigating if you're interested in properties for sale. You'll need to take a motorboat to see the developments on the other side of the lagoon. And be warned: Prices there have quadrupled in the last five years.

So down-to-earth is Utila that it has only one tourist resort (a second is in the works). The pleasant **Utila Lodge** (in the United States 800-282-8932), extending on stilts over the water, sits near the end of the main street. Dedicated to diving, it supplies excellent buffet meals coordinated with the aquatic schedule. Since the lodge has only eight guest rooms, reservations in season can be difficult to secure. The fee is $700 per person per week; non-divers should speak to Jim or Kisty Engel about lower off-season rates. Captain Ron, connected to the lodge, arranges day outings for sportfishermen with a fancy for marlin, tarpon, or snook.

You can almost always find a cheap room on Utila. Ask at any of the dive shops. Some shops have such close ties with guest houses that your room costs only a few dollars per day if you buy a diving package. About one-third of the 100 or so foreigners on the island are diving instructors. Diving rates, including certification, are lower here than on Roatán.

Hotel Utila (tel. 425-3340) is just a few steps beyond the Utila Lodge on the seaward side. Its 12 clean, motel-style double rooms have twin fans, private baths, and TV for $15 per person or $20 per couple. No meals are included, but owners Annie and Oneil Bush are currently building eight more rooms, a restaurant and lounge, and a dock for swimming. The tariff will probably be about double in the new addition. Annie boasts of 24-hour electricity; in most houses in town a flashlight is handy after midnight.

At the airport end of the main road is **Sharkey's Hotel**, tempting you to drop your bags there before venturing into town. Owner Althea Jackson offers 24-hour electricity and rooms with air-conditioning for $25. Only one room has a TV. If you like the convenience, look into renting one of her two comfortable efficiency apartments.

Also near the airport, **Trudy's** (tel. 425-3195) is a pleasant guest house with bright family-size rooms, owned by the same people who run the **Laguna del Mar** across the street, at which you can package food with lodging.

Utila is not noted for its cuisine. The fish, although fresh, is usually fried. The pastries and coconut bread are good with a distinct Caribbean flavor. The popular spot for breakfast is **Thomson's Bakery**, just off the main street, offering coffee and a variety of baked goods for $2 to $3. The **Mermaid** serves generous portions of tasty Italian dishes. The English-speaking proprietor will tell you about George Jackson's houses on nearby cays that up to six people can rent for $5 per day.

Near the airstrip and open all day is **Captain Roy's Bahia del Mar** where, for less than $5, you can choose from a varied menu (including vegetarian dishes) or lounge on the dock with a drink from the bar. The **Bucket of Blood** is another well-attended bar.

Before you leave Utila, you should try to meet two people. First, stop in at the **Green House Book Exchange** where you'll find Henrik Jensen, a Dane whose fluent English is only one of his half-dozen languages. He's a mine of information on Utila and the possibilities of renting or buying on the island.

The other island savant of my acquaintance is Anne Taylor, a charming and eloquent Australian who, with Brenda Thompson, edits and publishes the bimonthly *Utila Times*. This journal, Utila's answer to *The Coconut Telegraph*, carries 32 pages of news, oddities, sports, historical tidbits, and profiles of eccentrics, all dealing with

Utila, the "Flower of Honduras." Anne spins wonderful stories about native medicine and wisdom "intimate with the earth and the stars."

You may leave Utila with a twinge of regret. It somehow creates a nostalgia for a small village in a long-gone time—one that we never really knew.

The North Coast

La Ceiba

You can fly into the Golossón Airport from New York on Lacsa, Taca, or American Airlines, or from Miami on Taca, American, or Isleña. La Ceiba is serviced from the Bay Islands by Sosa, Isleña, or Lansa.

La Ceiba is the main jumping-off point for the Bay Islands. If you first arrive in July or August, you may also wish to visit the town of Esparta to the west to see the "crab invasion." Every year thousands of crabs scuttle through the town toward some unknown crustacean objective.

Because La Ceiba's streets follow a pattern, the central area is easy to get to know. Three main avenues run north and south: Republica, San Isidro, and 14 de Julio. Attempts at phonetic English equivalents are so inexact that, if you're short of Spanish, you're better off writing out addresses for your cab drivers. If your Spanish just needs a brush-up, **Eco-Escuela de Español** (tel. 443-2762) in La Ceiba offers instruction.

The east-west streets are numbered. First Street parallels the harbor, and the numbers rise as you move to the south-southeast. Extending north from Avenida Republica is the city pier and lighthouse. Broad sandy beaches lie to the east of the estuary, continuing toward the river, the Cangrejal.

The best beach is said to be Perú, at a fishing village about six miles outside town to the east. It has palm trees, grills, and roofed picnic tables for which you pay a nominal fee. Be aware that the beaches are somewhat risky at night.

Currency exchange is available at **Bancahsa** and at **Banco Atlantida**, two blocks north of the central park on San Isidro Avenue.

The **Banco Central** is to the east. An English-speaking travel agency is on the north side of the park. The official tourist center is on First Street, near the medical center. Another is on the south side of the park. You can rent a car from **Molinari** (tel. 443-0055) or from **Maya Rent A Car** (tel. 443-0224). **Hondutel** is below a radio tower east of the central park and above Sixth Street. The post office and **EMS Express Mail** lie to the southwest at Morazán Avenue and Thirteenth Street. Businesses open at 7 or 8 a.m. then shut down at 11 a.m. or noon; they open again from 2:30 to about 5 p.m.

In the shank of your first evening, go to the **Expatriates Bar**. You will find more foreigners here than anywhere else in the country. They will be a prime source of feedback on your questions. Owned by the jovial Mark Francis Fluellon and the winsome Maureen McNamara, to whom you should introduce yourself and explain your mission, this rooftop watering hole spreads dozens of tables around its long bar and out onto its open patio. On almost any evening you can get knowledgeable advice from at least a dozen expatriate residents. Tasty and surprisingly varied fare, mostly barbecue-style, is quickly served by

James D. Gollin

La Ceiba is another coastal paradise.

smiling young waitresses. (And well might they smile since they are said to make more in one night's tips than the typical Honduran job pays in a week.) The prices are decidedly lower than on Roatán (on my last visit I paid the equivalent of $4.50 for three gin-and-tonics, a vegetarian pizza on a tortilla, and a bottle of beer). Lively conversations surround you, and the polite newcomer is soon made to feel at home. If you end up leaving late, ask the armed watchman to find a cab and give him a small tip.

Hotel prices are surprisingly low compared to the resorts on the Bay Islands. Many hotels do not take credit cards, so be sure to exchange enough traveler's checks for cash to last several days. Almost all hotels provide safe-deposit boxes for your valuables and protected parking for rental cars. Rates listed are for double rooms with private bath. Singles are usually 20 to 25 percent lower.

Hotel La Quinta (tel. 443-0223, 443-0224, or 443-0225), new and large, wraps its rooms around well-tended small gardens and terraces, all centered around a pleasant pool. Carpeted, air-conditioned rooms with telephone and TV cost about $45. There are game and conference rooms and a "piano bar"—more accurately, guitar playing and a singer of Latin songs. The owner, Abdala Hitsaca, born in Bethlehem, Israel, emigrated after a heart operation and built the hotel.

Hotel El Colonial (tel. 443-1955) is new and convenient, with air-conditioned rooms with telephone and color TV for about $35. There's a restaurant, rooftop bar, sauna, and Jacuzzi, but no pool. The decor accords with the name.

Gran Hotel Paris (tel. 443-2391) is central but old and a bit faded. It does, however, have one of the town's better restaurants. Ask for one of the larger air-conditioned rooms by the clean, palm-shaded pool with a water slide. It will cost about $40.

Hotel Parthenon Beach (tel. 443-0404), on the beach east of the estuary, charges $35 for an air-conditioned room with a TV in the new wing facing the ocean. Suites cost an additional $25. A good restaurant and a car-rental agency are nearby.

Among restaurants, one excels. **Ricardo's**, run by a Honduran-American couple, has a charming garden terrace and an air-conditioned dining room. Beef, seafood, and pasta, beautifully prepared and well served with a grown-up wine card, make the $10 tab, higher than at most places, seem minuscule. Devotees pronounce Ricardo's food the best in all Honduras. The restaurant is closed Sundays.

El Portal opens early in the morning with novel sandwiches and Thai and Honduran dishes for $3 to $7. **2001** provides a beach setting under a thatched roof and serves charcoal-grilled fish and meats for $3 to $7. (By the way, there's a Laundromat next door where you can have about four pounds of clothes washed for $1.) Try the seafood crepes at the **Parthenon Beach Hotel** (see above). The roast chicken at **La Cumbre** is praiseworthy. **Pizza Hut** and **Burger King** have representative outlets, but with better service than in the States.

Dance halls (called discos) are numerous, majoring in rock and Latin rhythms. The Garifuna *punta* is frequent at the **Coco View**. The **Ocean Club** at the beach is owned by Americans. The *zona viva*, a concentration of nighttime activity, runs three blocks along First Street. Gambling is legal; a number of spots will take your money.

Trujillo

Getting to Trujillo is a bit of a problem. You can do it one way by renting a car in La Ceiba and driving. The trip is just over 160 kilometers (about two hours) on a paved two-lane highway with occasional potholes, washouts, and road repairs. Watch your odometer or you might miss the turnoff to Trujillo (Hondurans are casual about signposting).

Less stressful but somewhat slower is the bus for about $4. Buses leave about every hour from the terminal in La Ceiba. Try to get a through bus, and leave in the morning. If you leave too late you may find yourself overnighting in Tocoa, which offers very little. The North Coast Shuttle (see the "Communications and Transportation" chapter) is infrequent but faster and more comfortable. Expect to pay about $18.

Unfortunately you can't fly to Trujillo. There is an airstrip midway between the Christopher Columbus and Trujillo Bay hotels, but currently it is used only by private planes. Isleña used to land in

Trujillo twice a day but dropped the town from its schedule in 1996. The town is trying to get at least one flight a day restored.

Once you arrive, you'll find a pharmacy, hospital, post office, Hondutel, and the **Lavandería Colón**, where they'll wash and dry a bagful of clothes for $2. The **Banco de Occidente** cashes traveler's checks and lets you charge cash on your credit card. The police, their station situated adjacent to the central park, warn tourists that beaches are unsafe at night. There are taxis but they tend to disappear at nightfall. The town's noticeable jail was the first Honduran government house when Trujillo was the nation's first capital.

The central park, two blocks from the beach and facing the sea, is a good place to start your tour of the town. The **Iglesia y Catedral San Baptista**, a quaint, quasi-Gothic church of St. John the Baptist built in 1809, is open to viewing. A block away, the **Fort of Santa Barbara**, built in 1599 to repel pirates coveting gold shipments, allows visitors to stroll around its ancient walls, admire the old cannons on the bluff, and inspect exhibits in a former prison building

Remote Trujillo is known for its pristine beaches.

from 8 a.m. to 4 p.m. A modern hospital is next door. There's a tomb honoring William Walker nearby, but his actual burial place is in a fenced enclosure in the old cemetery to the west.

A ten-minute walk west past two other cemeteries leads to the odd but enjoyable **Museo y Piscina Riberas del Pedregal,** a huge private museum displaying archaeological finds, many of them Mayan, curious carvings, and eclectic miscellany—from ancient firearms to antiquated machinery. As the *Piscina* of the title suggests, there are a series of swimming pools fed by the Río Cristales and surrounded by bamboo shoots and tropical trees.

Three Garifuna villages lie from 8 to 12 miles along the dirt road to the west: Sante Fe, San Antonio, and the pretty Guadalupe, where an American is said to be building a retirement colony.

The **Trujillo Bay Hotel** (in the United States, 615-883-4770), managed by the amiable Jorge Brower, sits alongside the airstrip about 100 yards from the beach. New, pleasant, air-conditioned rooms for about $30 per night are all on one floor opening onto a shaded porch. The hotel's coffee shop–type restaurant with good food, great service, and a friendly atmosphere is patronized by a number of expatriate Americans.

Christopher Columbus Resort Hotel (tel. 434-4966 or in the United States 800-557-1492), although elegant and lavish, seems too determinedly posh for the colonial atmosphere of the town. Two green-and-white buildings house 70 colorful rooms with a view of the sea and all imaginable facilities. Rooms are $70; suites are $130.

Agua Caliente Hotel (tel. 434-4249), about 4 miles outside of (before) town, seems more in keeping with the environment. It has four hot spring–fed pools of sulfurous water, all thatch-covered with temperatures from about 70 to 104°F. If you're not a guest of the hotel, admission is $3. A sauna and massage cost a bit more. The hotel has seven cabins, each divided into two bright rooms ($45 each) with air-conditioning and TV.

Villas Brinkley (tel. 434-4444), reached by a rough dirt road and situated high on a hillside with a view of the bay, has large bright rooms with a Spanish-colonial feel. The hotel supplements its pool with health club facilities and boasts the only shuffleboard in all Honduras. There is a bar and restaurant but the latter has a full menu only for dinner. Call for current prices.

Hotel O'Glynn (tel. 434-4592), right in town near the central park, provides rooms with air-conditioning, TV, and balconies for about $26. It also has a roomy and comfortable lobby. The "O," honorific of the Irish name, is not genuine; it's a kind of standing joke between the owner and the town. Ask him about it.

Trujillo is scarcely the gourmet's lodestar. The food won't leave you hungry but it won't bring tears to your eyes either. **Praga** at the Agua Caliente Hotel serves dinner in air-conditioned comfort for $7 or less. It is named for the city of Prague in Czechoslovakia, where the Virgin of Medugorje is said to have made several miraculous appearances. For some private reason, the owner made a vow to build a church in honor of the Virgin. A votive offering, this beautiful white church is always empty, without priest or congregation. The hike to the church, up a steep hill and winding path past stations of the cross, is well worth the effort.

Trujillo's simple beachfront restaurants serve breakfast and fish. The **Perla del Caribe** is respected for its seafood soups and grilled shrimp and conch, all of which cost about $4. A lobster dinner runs about $8. The **Bar Bahia** is a good place to meet foreign residents. It's on the beach near the Christopher Columbus Resort. Prices range from $3 to $8 for a variety of dishes, including several vegetarian options. **Rincón de los Amigos** (The Friends' Corner), with its lively bar, is another expatriate hangout. The owner's special dinner—fish and half a lobster—is yours for $8.

If you're leaving Trujillo for San Pedro Sula, an outfit called Cotraipbal runs fast air-conditioned buses there. Or you can take the North Coast Shuttle.

Tela

Another coastal town, Tela, is west of La Ceiba. Unfortunately, there's only one decent road into Tela from the highway, and it's hard to find if you're driving. Instead, if you are in La Ceiba, you can take a fast air-conditioned Catisa bus bound for San Pedro Sula. Pay

the full $2 fare, but tell the driver you'd like to be dropped off at
Tela. He'll leave you on the highway; from there a dollar will pay for
a taxi into town.

Tela's central park is on 9ª Street between 5ª and 6ª Avenues.
(Those odd little "a"s come from the Spanish ordinal numbers—
quinta, *sesta*, etc.—and correspond to our "th"s as in 5th and 6th.)
Prolansate is a kind of tourist office and sells maps and tours.
Bancahsa is open five and a half days a week. The pharmacy and the
bus terminal are nearby. Two blocks inland, along 7ª Street, are the
post office, Hondutel with fax and phone, a clinic, and a laundry.
Because United Fruit long had a piece of this town, English is fairly
widely spoken.

Villas Telemar (in the United States 800-742-4276) is certainly
worth a visit, whether you stay there or not. It's actually a good-sized
village all by itself. Built to shelter the families of United Fruit exec-
utives, now long gone, the resort offers air-conditioned rooms with
hardwood floors, high ceilings, and abundant plants, as well as furnished apartments and cottages on stilts. At $66 for a double or $80
for a suite with a kitchenette and a living-dining room, the place is a
great value. A splendid beach, two pools, tennis courts, and golf are
free of extra charge to all guests. Horseback riding, fishing, and
waterskiing can be arranged. There's a good restaurant and bar and
even a small zoo. If you don't stay here, you can still use all the facilities for a $2 fee.

Hotel Sherwood (tel. 448-2416) is rather plain, but it offers
beachfront rooms with air-conditioning, telephone, and cable TV, as
well as a bar and restaurant, for about $40 per night. **Ejuciutivos
Apart-Hotel** (tel. 448-2047), a whitewashed building, is businesslike
and roomy and just a four-block walk from the beach. It's worth its
$32 per night, but you can't charge your room. **The Last Resort** (tel.
448-2545) is located a few miles to the west of town in the partly
Garifuna village of Tornabé. It has bungalows and a great wooden
terrace on the lagoon and a decent low-priced restaurant. For $80
you can get a five-bed bungalow.

The **Marabu Inn** is an excellent restaurant on the beach
between the center of town and Telemar Villas. Patrons eat in a

large, fan-cooled room in a private house. Meals known for their remarkably delicate and inventive seasoning cost between $4 and $6.

Uraguay al Sur lives up to its name in the way it grills its meats. Seafood is also well served in the air-conditioned dining room or on the outdoor terrace. Prices run from $3 to $8. The restaurant is just across the street from the Telemar Villas.

At the beach and open evenings only, **The Sherwood** offers a variety of juices in addition to cold and hot seafood dishes, almost all for $6 or less. Nearby, **Casa Azul** has a bar, an art gallery, and Italian dishes for $4 or less.

While in Tela, nature-lovers, garden-growers, and bird-watchers will want to take a three-mile taxi trip to the **Jardín Botánico Lancetilla**. This former experimental station for crop diversification, now a Honduran preserve, flaunts thousands of species of trees and plants. One ghastly variety is the strychnine tree: so toxic as to be untouchable, so deadly that it kills any birds that peck at it. Keep your eye on the color-coded tags; black means poison. The best time to visit these world-class gardens is early morning. An extra dividend on your $5 admission is the presence of clouds of birds. A tree nursery, a research laboratory, and an extensive biological reserve adjoin the arboretum.

Also a must-see is the **Punta Sal Marine National Park**, about 14 miles west of Tela near the Garifuna villages. Reached by tour boats or a hike from the village of Miami, this protected area of about 155 square miles is a cluster of ecosystems embracing idyllic beaches, muddy savannas, reefs and shipwrecks, rocky cliffs and tranquil lagoons, and a wide assortment of flora and fauna. On the way to the park you'll pass Monkey Lagoon, a choice spot for bird-watchers. Neither place has an admission charge.

Puerto Cortés

Puerto Cortés can be reached by train from Tela and San Pedro Sula about twice a week, if you don't mind five hours of dust and noise. The scenery, glimpsed through grimy windows, is reported to be attractive. The fruit companies turned over the railway years ago when they began using trucks and shipping containers instead. You can also bus to the port from San Pedro Sula, changing at Progresso, but the ride's not much better than that offered by the train.

The port has some fine beaches, a lively central plaza, a couple of nearby Garifuna villages, and miles of frantically busy shipping installations on the bay. If you are investment-minded and already weighing shipping problems, perhaps you should visit this town, the major port of Honduras and the equal of any port in Central America. But be sure to bring a poncho or an umbrella, for it's very rainy.

If you must stay overnight here, the favored hotel is the oddly spelled **Hotel Mister Ggeer** (tel. 555-0444), with air-conditioning, TV, and a restaurant for about $40. You can get a decent buffet lunch there, or try **Fronteras del Caribe** or the **Playa Azul** for seafood.

The Two Capitals

Last but not least on most itineraries are the two capitals: San Pedro Sula, the financial capital, and Tegucigalpa (Tegus), the political.

James D. Gollin

Jardín Botánico Lancetilla is home to exotic plants.

San Pedro Sula

Arriving in San Pedro on an international flight, you can take advantage of the duty-free shop then grab a taxi to almost anywhere in the city for about $6. Aeorhonduras and Taca fly regularly from Tegus. Isleña, Sosa, and Caribbean Air connect with La Ceiba and the Bay Islands. Fast modern buses also link this city with all the principal destinations. Because of this, tourists often use this city as a center for departures elsewhere: Copán, Tegucigalpa, the North Coast, or the Gulf of Fonseca.

Downtown San Pedro Sula is

extremely easy to navigate. The avenues run north-south; the streets run east-west. The city center is at First Avenue and First Street, and helpful signs tell you how far you are from that point. A ring road (Avenida Circunvalación) loops around the downtown grid.

You won't find a great variety of activities, nor does the city seem interested in becoming a magnet for casual visitors. But the living is pleasant here, even if the lodging is a bit high priced. All hotels have two sets of prices, one rate for tourists and a discounted rate for Hondurans or resident foreigners. It's not a breach of etiquette to ask for a discount.

Gran Hotel Sula (tel. 552-7000 or in the United States 800-223-6767), one of the two large and lavish hostelries in the city, is conveniently located on First Street alongside the central park. Although built in the fifties, its maintenance, comforts, service, and facilities are excellent. A double costs about $100, but you get your money's worth. Suites with kitchenettes are available. The air-conditioned rooms come with coffeemakers, balconies, and color TVs fed by satellite. (Most of the films are in English with Spanish subtitles, a good means of brushing up on your Spanish orthography.) Chambermaids service the rooms twice daily. A charming tiled courtyard with fountains adjoins the pool. There is a business center with secretarial help and all needed electronic gadgetry, a health club, casino, 24-hour coffee shop, bar, and restaurant.

Hotel Copantl Sula (tel. 553-0900 or 556-7180) is the grand hotel of San Pedro Sula and perhaps of all Honduras. Set on spacious grounds in the southern suburbs with guarded parking, its soaring three-story lobby, hung with baskets and lighted spheres, is impressive. It also serves as the town's country club with its Olympic-size eight-lane pool, tennis and handball courts, sauna, Jacuzzi, exercise room, and massage facilities. A double room—spotless, carpeted, air-conditioned, and equipped with color TV—costs just under $100. A bank, several shops, a casino, three restaurants, and a coffee shop are on the premises, from which a free bus leaves every half hour to shuttle guests into town.

Hotel-Suites Los Andes (tel. 557-0471), at about $70 per unit, is a complex of small furnished apartments on the ring road. It's a good place to stay if you're spending time in the city on business. Apartments include a small bedroom joined to a kitchenette with a dishwasher. TV and air conditioning are included. A terrace, pool, whirlpool bath, garden, convenience store, coffee shop, restaurant, and bar are on the premises.

Hotel International Palace (tel. 557-6824), not far from the center and fairly new, provides foam mattresses and tiled bathrooms along with air conditioning, TV, and private balconies for about $45.

Javier's House (tel. 557-6322 or in the United States 800-553-2513), about a mile southwest of the center, is an American-style bed-and-breakfast with an English-speaking owner. Rooms cost $45. Ideal for a hit-and-run visit.

Good eating is not too difficult to find. For breakfast, lunch, or a light late snack at budget prices, the **Skandia**, a first-floor café in the Gran Hotel Sula, is a winner. Go up one flight at the same hotel for a first-class generous buffet lunch for $7 at the **Granada**, or dine on excellent continental fare at the same restaurant for about $10. Equally excellent cuisine is to be had at the **Copantl Sula**, but you'll pay a bit more. For a slab of beef or a surf-and-turf for $10, check out **Pat's Steak House** nearby. **José y Pepe's** provides an excellent taste of Mexico for $7 to $12 in an upstairs air-conditioned room.

Departing from San Pedro Sula, you have a choice of many destinations. If you've rented a car, here are the distances in both kilometers and miles:

to	kilometers	miles
Trujillo	373	233
Tela	99	62
Puerto Cortés	64	40
La Ceiba	202	126
Choluteca	374	234
Copán ruins	170	106
Tegucigalpa	241	151

More economical eating is found in such Chinese restaurants as the **Copa de Oro, Taiwan,** and **Lucky,** or in the Italian **Vicente,** all averaging less than $6 for dinner. *Pincho*s, a kind of shish kebab, cost about $2 at **Mackies,** a pleasant open-air spot. **Wendy's, Pizza Hut,** and **Burger King** nestle close to the car-free shopping block.

If you decide to drive to Tegucigalpa, make at least a short visit to Siguatepeque (see the "Prime Living Choices" chapter). If the town captures your fancy enough to make you stay a while, the **Hotel International Gomez** and the **Zari** are comfortable enough at about $9.

Tegucigalpa

Many international airlines include Tegucigalpa on their runs. Besides the familiar American, Continental, Lacsa, and Taca, there are European carriers including Iberia, Alitalia, KLM, and Lufthansa. Tegucigalpa's runway is well maintained but very short, forcing planes to dive suddenly before they land. Takeoffs are less nerve-racking because they require less runway. There is talk of moving the airport to Comayagua for safety. Perhaps those tentative plans account for the minimal facilities at the present airport. There's a post office that closes at 3 p.m. and phones at the Hondutel office. Outside the terminal a cluster of cab drivers will compete for the privilege of driving you to almost any destination in town for $5. (Budget travelers with little luggage often walk about 300 yards out to the main road and flag passing taxis for half the price.) There's a bank at the airport, but the money-changers out front often offer better rates.

Budget and Toyota rent cars at the terminal, but you probably shouldn't drive in Tegucigalpa. Rent when you are leaving for another city or town, but use taxis in the capital. They're inexpensive and drivers know their way around.

There is no central bus terminal. Fast modern buses leave for San Pedro Sula and La Ceiba. The desk clerk at your hotel can advise you where to find them. Taking local buses within the city poses almost insuperable difficulties. They are identified by the barrios through which they wander along mysterious ways.

Before you leave your hotel, purchase the latest copy of *Honduras*

This Week, a mine of information about the country, supplemented by international news. The paper reviews new hotels, restaurants, and travel services. Ads suggest hotels, restaurants, and entertainment of interest to the tourist. Also buy the latest copy of the quarterly *Honduras Tips*. Although it focuses on Copán, it is packed with advice on lodging, food, services, and sights in all the major cities and towns. Its alternating pages of English and Spanish will give you a chance to brush up on your Spanish vocabulary.

Ironically, Tegucigalpa's poor-cousin city, Comayaguela, has an understandable grid of streets, while the capital resembles a web woven by a disoriented spider. The streets and avenues are named but only partially numbered, numbered streets are also called avenues, and sometimes streets intersect at unexpected angles. As you walk north on an avenue, the street numbers, if you can find them, go up. Walking along a street, the avenue numbers rise as you go east.

The small downtown area, with the bulk of the tourist sights, centers on the Plaza Morazán, often called Central Park and containing

James D. Gollin

San Pedro Sula's Central Park

an inauthentic statue of the national hero. Even if the equestrian statue is fraudulent, swarms of patriotic birds descend on his square at sunset and serenade him. You can reach this square from most hotels for $3 or less by taxi. If you make this square your focal point you should be able to walk around with some confidence.

Halfway down the park on the west side is the three-block **Calle Peatonal** (Pedestrian Street), devoted to shops and stalls. Continuing west for two blocks, you'll come to the **Iglesia Los Dolores** (its approximate English rendering would be Church of the Sorrows of the Virgin), nearly 250 years old with a gold-plated altar, soaring blue and gold dome, and extraordinary decorative touches inside and out. A public market spreads its skirts nearby.

A bit to the west is the **National Palace**, housing the Ministry of Foreign Affairs. Nearby is the post office, once an orphanage. Just to the south is the **Bancahsa** for changing traveler's checks or obtaining a cash advance on your credit card. **Hondutel**, with its phone, fax, and telegram services, is also located here.

Crossing Third Avenue you'll find the national theater (**Teatro Nacional Manuel Bonilla**) down a side street, pink outside and gold and white in its double-horseshoe interior. Built before World War I and painstakingly restored, the theater stages performances and concerts regularly. Across the little park is the eighteenth-century **Calvary Church**.

If your energy level is high, a stroll four blocks north will bring you to **Concordia Park** with its imitations of Mayan stelae, a miniature replica of the Chichén Itzén temple in the Yucatán, and a small botanical garden with a Lake of Love and a Bridge of Sighs—modeled after the famous Venetian bridge.

The police station is near the park. As evidence of the easing of Ladino machismo, there is also a Policia Femenina, staffed entirely by women and specializing in the problems of women and children. Up a steep hill in a large mansion you'll find the **National Museum** (closed on Monday and Tuesday and at 3:30 p.m. other days). The ethnology section is particularly interesting, depicting the daily lives and customs of indigenous Honduran tribes. Other sections deal with the colonial period, Paleolithic findings, ancient Mayan objects, and carved pieces of gems, obsidian, and jade.

Across from the southeast corner of the central park rise the twin towers of **Catedral de San Miguel de Tegucigalpa**, flaunting pleated columns and mermaid pillars. Inside are a remarkable pulpit, altarpieces plated in gold and silver, and some very old religious paintings. Two blocks to the east is the **Museo del Hombre Hondureño** (Museum of the Honduran Man), mostly paintings and photos of local scenes from various periods. A bookstore specializing in Honduran matters is almost next door. A few steps beyond is the **Church of St. Francis**, the oldest in the city, founded by the Franciscans but altered in 1740 when somewhat Moorish touches were insinuated into its original simplicity. With luck you may get a peek at colonial-era painting and the gold-plated altar.

A zigzag walk southwest from the central park may offer the most varied sights. Go south on Bolivar Street to a small park fronting the seventeenth-century **Iglesia La Merced** (Mercy Church), with a number of colonial paintings and a showpiece altar. The green building in the park, formerly the home of the National University, is soon to be the **National Gallery of Arts**. A jog to the right takes you to the **National Congress**, unmistakable because its modern building rests on metal stilts, leaving an open area beneath. If you wish to cross west to Sixth Avenue you will see a grandiose structure, popularly called the **Wedding Cake**. Somewhat Moorish in style and fortresslike in construction, this used to be the pink Presidential Palace, but now, in a more modest beige, it houses the **Museum of the History of the Republic**. The president's offices have been moved to a suburb. The Honduran Institute of Tourism, a good source of maps, maintains a desk in the museum.

Glancing south you'll see the **Puente Mallol** (pronounced MA-yole), the oldest bridge in the city. If you cross it into Comayaguela, go south to Second Street then west until you come to the **San Isidro Market**, the largest in the city, sprawling over several blocks. Here you'll find a flood of food, cheap industrial goods, and some handicrafts. You can bargain with the vendors without offending them. The area is safe, but beware of pickpockets. A bit farther along, a market specializing in handicrafts opens on weekends. Neither in the market nor in the capital itself is strolling alone at random after dark advisable.

Hotel Honduras Maya (tel. 232-5191 or in the United States 800-448-8355) is the town's top hotel in more ways than one with its 12 floors and Maya-inspired frieze. At about $100 to $130 for the corporate rate, you get all the expected comforts with a complimentary buffet breakfast and free local phone calls. A large heated pool, health club, several restaurants, coffee shop, convention facilities, and protected parking are also included. There's also a casino with blackjack and one-armed bandits. The British consulate and the American Express offices are within a stone's throw. The hotel is on the Avenida de Chile.

Hotel Plaza San Martín (tel. 237-2928), in a big and new blockhouse with terraces, offers balconied rooms with the comforts you'd expect at a price only about $15 lower than the Maya's. The lack of a pool may account for the reduction. The hotel is just east of downtown.

Hotel Plaza (tel. 237-2111) is modern, friendly, and right in the center of things, opposite the post office. Queen-size beds in air-conditioned rooms with TV and desks are priced at about $65. There's no swimming pool, but the hotel is a good value.

Gran Hotel Krystal (tel. 237-8804) is in the center of town and a favorite of Honduran businessmen who don't mind that the rooms, although complete with the things you'd expect, are modest and rather dark. A good place to meet the natives in their natural habitat, this one is a bargain at about $30.

Hotel restaurants serve American food for prices under $10 for dinner. In this city a beer will add between $1 and $1.25 to your meal, a soft drink about 60 cents. The local rum is cheap, but imported liquor or wine may put a dent in your budget. The coffee shop at the **Hotel Krystal** is a bargain. The meals are varied and good although unsurprising for a top price of about $5.

For charcoal-grilled meats, the ranch-style **La Terraza de Don Pepe** keeps prices at about $5. **Al Natural** near the central park

offers an inner courtyard and serves mostly vegetarian food and sal-
ads for $3 to $4 until closing at 7 p.m. There are several fast-food
establishments in the area: a **Burger King**, a copycat **Burger Hut**,
and several pizzerias near the central park.

If you stroll along the Boulevard Morazán, you'll find yourself
surrounded by eating places, varied in type and price. Afterward take
in a film. No addresses are given in the theater ads. You have to ask
at your hotel for the locations. Nonsmokers may also find it troublesome that smoking is allowed in the movie houses.

When you leave town, don't pin everything on a precise hour or
even a day of departure. Check the weather forecast the night
before; the regional airlines don't fly in the rain.

One more thing: Don't drink the water in Tegucigalpa unless it's
bottled. The American embassy has declared the local water unsafe
for the tourist.

Comayagua

Along the highway just 53 miles north of Tegucigalpa, you'll find
the city of Comayagua. It elbowed its way in for mention here not as
a retirement town but because it was for over three centuries the
country's capital. I'd never wish to retire there, and it's fairly far
down even on my visiting list. An interest in art and architecture
may draw you there, however. A bus from either San Pedro Sula or
Tegus will drop you off near the Texaco station on the highway, from
which it's a ten-minute walk into town.

There are some fine colonial buildings still standing and recently
restored; many of the earliest were burned by a Guatemalan army or
flattened by a quake two centuries ago. Several churches are of venerable age, especially **Mercy Church** (Iglesia La Merced). The
Cathedral of Comayagua, dedicated to the Immaculate Conception
and rebuilt from the ground up in 1708, is impressive. Facing the
central park, the facade is an ornately carved set of sculpted figures
above the doorway: four church fathers, Joseph and John the Baptist
and, above them all, Christ with outstretched hands. Columns run
up the height of the building. The interior is royally rich. Among

the paintings is a martyrdom scene by Murillo. Jutting out of one side of the cathedral is a buttressed bell tower topped by a colorful cupola housing one of the oldest working clocks in the world. Built by Moors in twelfth-century Spain, this clock was removed from the Alhambra in Granada and given by Philip II to the town's first cathedral. Almost as ancient an object is the bell in the **Church of San Francisco,** cast in 1464.

If even older objects engage you, walk a block to an interesting collection of pre-Columbian art and artifacts in the archaeological museum (**Museo de Arqueología**), closed Monday and Tuesday. Religious objects are housed in the **Museo Colonial.**

One excursion, farther north on the highway between San Pedro Sula and Tegucigalpa, may be rewarding. **Lake Yojoa** offers beauty and a host of pleasant pastimes. The hotels by the lake provide equipment rentals and serve good food at reasonable prices. One, the **Brisas del Lago,** at near resort prices, offers tennis courts and a dance hall. If you're a lake lover, stay a while. You may find it an attractive place to reside.

Copán

If you're ever near the northwest of the country, you'll surely want to see the great Mayan mystery of Copán. There are only three practical ways to get to the ruins: take a bus, drive yourself, or take a tour. There used to be an airstrip for air taxis, but it's no longer in service. A new museum is being built over part of the former strip.

In any case, I suggest you start from San Pedro Sula. If busing or driving, make clear to everyone you encounter that your objective is Copán Ruinas, not Santa Rosa de Copán, a quite different town, reached by another fork in the road and some 25 miles south of the ruins.

The road is in good shape with rises and sways as you climb about 1,000 feet into the beginnings of coffee and cacao country. In the rainy season, watch for washouts and flooded areas. An outfit called Adventure Shuttle (tel. 557-2380) charges $18 each way for a two and a half-hour air-conditioned van ride. The Etumi bus company runs two direct buses daily—an hour or so before and after noon—which make the trip in about three hours at less than half that price. They return early the next morning. Public buses run by Empresa de Transportes Torito leave almost every hour for Santa Rosa de Copán. If you wish to travel with them you must change at La Entrada, at a fork about 20 miles before the highway reaches Copán. With the change, the trip is close to five hours, so don't plan to return the same day.

The easiest and best way to go is by tour. MC Tours (tel. 898-3070 or 3072) or Maya Tropic Tours (tel. 552-2405 or 552-5401) will transport you in a comfortable van in about two and a half hours each way, provide an English-speaking driver and guide, take you on a three-hour tour through the ruins and the museum, put you up in a first-class hotel, and sometimes provide a box lunch, all for $135.

By comparison, if you go by bus, you'll have to walk to the ruins or hire local transportation (the ruins are 1 kilometer east of the town), hire a guide for about $25, and pay your $3 admission. You may also have to stay at less desirable lodgings. If you do it on your own the total cost will be about half that of the tour, but will require negotiations every step of the way.

The town itself is a colonial charmer. It's nestled in a small valley among hills, and temperatures are cooler than on the coast. Cobblestoned streets lead past pastel buildings with tiled roofs to a central park and a church on its east side. The name Copán is historically a misnomer. Speaking Nahuatl, guides told Spanish invaders the place was called Copantl, or "Wooden Bridge Area," but since each language has consonants unknown to the other, the Spanish shortened the name to Copán.

The town's population is small, but there seems to be a disproportionate number of light-footed boys who, if you know a little Spanish, are eager to solve your problems, arrange for rental of a saddle horse, or run your errands for a few lempiras. There are no beggars, no fruit vendors, and no fast-food stands. Almost all services—bank, post office, Hondutel, Laundromat, pharmacy, and a medical clinic—are within a block of the town square.

A new development nearby hopes to lure foreign retirees to the simple life in the area. Town life here would be easy but uneventful. There are thermal baths at Agua Caliente, a 45-minute drive along a dirt road, and a great bird-watching spot in the Peña Quemada reserve, about 14 miles distant.

Also on the town square, and not to be missed, is the **Copán Regional Museum,** offering a representative collection of artifacts found at the site. A reconstruction of a scribe's burial site demonstrates that intellectual accomplishments were highly regarded by the ancients. A sculptured bench from a house excavated at Las Sepulturas gives an indication of furnishings in a middle-class home of the times. You'll see jade jewelry, knives of obsidian, a skull with a tooth and jade filling, an arresting sculpture of a mourning woman, a prurient bat, sacrificial blood, and whole stelae brought inside to protect them from further erosion. In one room lie the skeletal remains of a Mayan buried with his pet turtles. Bodies were placed in the fetal position, presumably to ease later rebirth into the otherworld.

James D. Gollin

The ruins at Copán are not to be missed.

If you visit the museum first, note that the $3 entrance ticket is valid for two days and is good also for admission to the main ruins and to Las Sepulturas. Conversely, a ticket purchased at the entrance to the ruins offers reciprocal privileges.

There's a language school in town where you can take Spanish lessons at very reasonable prices. The **Escuela de Español Ixbalanque** (Ish-bah-lan-keh) offers one-on-one instruction in a town where few residents speak English.

Hotel Marina Copán (tel. 898-3480 or 898-3070), a former estate converted to a gracious resort in colonial style, offers gardens and a pool between passageways floored and roofed with red tile. The property includes a sauna, tennis courts, bar, and a picturesque restaurant. The hotel is usually part of the package with MC Tours. A double room costs $75 if you're on your own.

Hotel Madrugada (tel. 898-3092) is easier on the budget. Comfortable rooms ($42) come with showers and ceiling fans, and dinner is served by an English-speaking staff. **Los Jaguares** (tel. 898-3075) is colorful, comfortable, and convenient for $37.

The restaurant at the marina has the most varied menu with breakfasts and lunches for about $4 and dinners for about $10. Easier on the budget but good are the **Tankul, La Llama del Bosque,** and **Los Gauchos.** For more dining options, consult *Honduras Tips.*

If your Spanish is serviceable, mosey down to the towns of **Santa Rosa de Copán** and **La Esperanza** (see the "Prime Living Choices" chapter). In the former, Hotel Elvir will house you and arrange trips in the area for very reasonable prices. In La Esperanza lodging is inexpensive, about $10 per day in simple rooms with private baths at either the Solis or Gomez Hotels. Alternatively, for another peek at a distant past, drive four kilometers from La Entrada to the newly opened archaeological site at **El Puente.** The ruins are considered second only to those in Copán, and the town's museum of anthropology is excellent. The **El San Carlos Hotel** is comfortable and inexpensive.

The Gulf Area

If you are curious about the Pacific rim of Honduras, follow Highway CA1 south from Tegucigalpa. At Jicaro Galán you will intercept the Pan American Highway on its brief 100-mile run through the Honduran lowlands from El Salvador to Nicaragua. This bypass, by avoiding the mountains, has kept the great highway from the capital and other major cities of Honduras and is partly responsible for the late development of the country.

A stop nine miles before the highway juncture, at the picturesque village of **Perspire,** offers a triple-domed church, a handsome town hall, an unspoiled colonial town paved in stone, and a burbling river—but no tourist accommodations. If you follow the road west through Nacaome (hot springs and a colonial church) you will soon find yourself at the Salvadorian border.

If, however, you continue south along the highway to the port town of San Lorenzo, you can ferry to **Ampala** on the **Isla del Tigre** (Tiger Island), the only town on the islands of the Gulf of Fonseca. Ampala was once the major Honduran port but now it's a ghost town, its vitality drained by bustling San Lorenzo, which not only handles container shipping but is also the center of the booming shrimp-farming industry. You can climb an inactive volcano on Tiger Island or swim in the warm gulf water, but the beaches are somewhat coarse with dark volcanic sand.

Continuing on the highway to the southeast, you will arrive at **Choluteca**, the biggest city in southern Honduras. In the center of a large valley nourished by rivers and streams, this market town serves the flourishing agricultural and livestock activity around it, a belt of fertility rare in Honduras. Like a scene out of the Old West, ox carts heaped with melons trundle by as cowboys (*gauchos*) herd cattle or lead strings of pack animals. About a quarter mile from the town center you'll find the colonial neighborhood of **Parque Valle**. A feast of colonial architecture, it includes the restored home of one of the signers of Central America's declaration of independence.

For the Adventurous

Visiting the great national parks and protected areas of Honduras is adventure in itself. But one area is particularly challenging. In the far northeast of the country lies the Mosquitia, hundreds of miles of swampy savannas and seemingly impenetrable rain-soaked jungles, rivers, rapids, and marshy estuaries, sparsely populated by scattered aboriginal tribes clinging to age-old customs and cultures. There are places here that will enable you to reread Joseph Conrad's *Heart of Darkness* with a new understanding.

Since the only practical modes of transportation are by small plane and canoe, and since you'll need a guide unless you opt for a tour group, a trip there of any length will cost about as much as you'd spend in Bay Island resorts over the same time period. But those who do visit the Mosquitia begrudge not a penny of expense, claiming the experience to be a treasured memory. To Jim McDonnell—16 years an investor resident, a bush pilot who hauls conchs and cargo to and from the Mosquitia—the whole area, including his little offshore island, is paradise. He speaks with great affection of the aboriginal Indians and delights in relating bits of their folklore.

Sosa and Isleña Airlines operate regular flights to Palacio or to Puerto Lempira on the Caratasca Lagoon for about $40. Or you could pay a bush pilot in La Ceiba to fly you to one of those villages or to an airstrip farther in. Then you'll set off on your own, after brushing up on your snake identification, loading up on camping equipment, renting a dugout, and hiring a guide—trusting in the missionaries you meet to put you up nights. Commercial lodgings are virtually nonexistent in the interior. Personally, I'm in favor of letting a tour group handle the whole thing.

The entire region is a reserve. The **Biosphere of the Plátano** is a special attraction, full of diverse wildlife, including six-foot storks, giant butterflies, and the Tawahka, a Sumo Indian group who have maintained traditions from the Stone Age. Honduras is trying to maintain the ecological and anthropological integrity of the area and

James D. Gollin

Tiger Island in the Gulf of Fonseca

so regulates the companies it allows to operate tours there. In Tegucigalpa, contact La Moskitia Ecoaventuras (tel. 237-9398) or Trek de Honduras (tel. 238-1944); in Trujillo, Cambia C.A. (tel. 552-7335).

The tour companies usually tell you what to bring. Be sure to take plenty of insect repellent, a flashlight, and a pancho for river rafting, and continue to take your twice-weekly antimalarial pills, which you should start a week or two before.

Another possibility is to join a caravan and pursue the track of the ancient Mayas through Honduras and Guatemala. A ten-day tour, starting from San Pedro Sula, is offered by Aventuras Centroamericanas (tel. 553-2372). On this trip, an experienced bilingual guide leads a string of four-by-fours first to Copán, then to Caracol in Belize and Tikál and Quirigua in Guatemala. The tour also visits several newly discovered pre-Columbian archaeological sites. In some areas you'll hike or paddle a canoe, but most of the time you'll drive. You'll plunge through one of the world's last remaining rain forests, shower in waterfalls, relax in hot springs, and mosey through forgotten Spanish colonial villages, dreaming away like the town in *Brigadoon*. The all-inclusive cost is $1,200.

And So, Adieu

To my age-mates all, may the fortuitous be with you! I too am in the gold-watch generation. Personal obligations keep me stateside for now, but I love Honduras and will someday be a visa veteran or a roving resident. To you would-be investors, good luck wherever you decide to lay a bet. But mull over the possibility that Honduras may be the next Latin bull market.

Appendix

HELPFUL PUBLICATIONS

Local Papers
Coconut Telegraph (Roatan)
Honduras Tips (San Pedro Sula)
Utila Times (Bay Islands)

Books
The Cruising Guide to the Honduras Bay Islands, Westcott Cobe
    Publishers
Diving and Snorkeling Roatán and Honduras Bay Islands, by Sharon
    Collins, Libreria Casi Todo
Honduras: A Country Study, Library of Congress
Honduras: Adventures in Nature, by James D. Gollin and Ron
    Mader, John Muir Publications
Honduras: The Owner's Manual, International Living

Other Publications
Honduras: Central American Adventure Magazine
International Living

FOR MORE INFORMATION

International Living
Agora Inc.
105 W. Monument St.
Baltimore, MD 21291
(410) 223-2611

TOUR COMPANIES

In the United States:
American Tours and Travel (206) 623-8850
Discovery Tours (800) 926-6575 or (561) 243-6276
Great Trips (800) 552-3419
Honduras Travel (212) 972-6867
Roatán Charters (800) 282-8932
Visit Central America Program (800) 255-8222

In Honduras:
Ecohonduras (443-0933)
Euro Honduras (443-0933)
Explore Honduras (552-6239)
Garifuna Tours (448-2904)
Hondu Maya (558-1059)
La Moskitia Ecoaventuras (237-9398)
Mayan VIP Tours (553-4672)
MC Tours (553-3076)
Ríos Honduras/Caribbean Travel Agency (443-0780)

TABLE OF METRIC CONVERSIONS

The first three columns below are of use when you have a pencil and paper or a calculator at hand. The "sloppy" column will give you fair accuracy when you are on the street or in your car and must perform the calculations in your head.

from	multiply by	to find	or	(sloppy way)
centimeters	0.39	inches		multiply by 2 and divide by 5
meters	3.28	feet		add $1/4$ number to triple the number
kilometers	0.621	miles		double number and divide by 3
square meters	10.755	square feet		add a 0 to the number
square meters	1.195	square yards		add $1/5$ number to number
hectares	2.47	acres		double number and add $1/2$ number
liters	0.946	quarts		a quart equals a liter
liters	0.26	gallons		divide number by 4
kilograms	2.2	pounds		double number

Conversely,
1 gallon = 3.78 liters
1 pound = 0.454 grams
1 mile = 1.61 kilometers
3.28 feet = 1 meter
1 inch = 2.54 centimeters

GLOSSARY OF TERMS

Bay Islands (Islas de la Bahía): A group of islands off the North Coast of Honduras, including the largest islands of Roatán, Utila, and Guanaja

casas de cambio: exchange houses (places to exchange money)

centavo: 1/100 of a lempira

Copán: The site of ruins of a major Mayan city in western Honduras

Daddy Warbucks investor: A foreign investor who pledges one million lempiras toward establishing a business in Honduras

Decree 80-92: Capstone of the new policy welcoming foreign investment

Decree 93-91: The principal Honduran law dealing with foreign pensionates and rentists

dispensa: The right of pensionates and rentists (and their dependents who are not investors) to bring their household furnishings to Honduras, exempt from customs duties and import taxes

estadounidense: Literally, a "United Stateser"; a citizen of the United States

FIDE: Foundation for Investments and Development of Exports (also known as the Industrial Development Group-Honduras); a nonprofit organization dedicated to nurturing the development of Honduran business

Free Zones: The cities of Puerto Cortés, Omoa, Choloma, Tela, La Ceiba, and Ampala. Export companies operating in these zones may import material, equipment, and office supplies without duties, and they are exempt from taxes. The companies may repatriate money without restriction.

Garifunas: Black Caribs; descendants of African slaves who intermarried with natives on the island of St. Vincent and were later deported to the Bay Islands. Garifunas still live on the Bay Islands and on Honduras's Caribbean coast

Hondutel: Government-run offices offering phone, fax, and internet services

jubilado: A retiree who has passed his 65th birthday

Ladino: A person of mestizo descent; the Honduran mestizo culture

lempira: The Honduran unit of currency. As of April 1998, the rate of exchange was 13.19L for $1.

mestizo: A person of mixed European and American Indian ancestry

Mosquitia: The Mosquito Coast in far northeast Honduras, characterized by swampy savannas, jungles, rivers, rapids, and marshy estuaries

personalismo: The Honduran regard for family and the individual

Private Export Processing Zones: Zones in which companies pay no taxes and no customs duties on imported materials or exported products. Companies also face no restrictions on the use of foreign exchange or repatriation of capital or profits.

punta: The traditional Garifuna dance-song

rentist: A foreign resident of independent means

Third Age (Tercera Edad): Legislation describing government benefits for Hondurans over age 65

Tourist Free Zone Law: a law that exempts tourist businesses from income tax on profits and sales tax on building materials. The law also allows for the duty-free import of materials and equipment, including motor vehicles, boats, and airplanes used in the tourist trade.

Index

Map Index

About the Author

Frank Ford, father of eight and a veteran of World War II, has written plays and several television shorts and has acted in television, theater, and films. He has taught English at various colleges and universities and has worked as a consultant for Metropolitan Life and International Paper.

He has traveled in North and Central America and in Europe as far east as Turkey. He has lived in Guatemala, selling textiles, night-guarding the embassy, reporting news in English, and tutoring a local debutante until a revolution blew away his kitchen and bedroom.

Among his fondest travel memories are those of roaming through Honduras, delighting in the companionship of the Honduran expatriates whom he interviewed in preparation for this book. Now retired, Ford lives on Long Island.